Linguistic Description in English for Academic Purposes

This volume provides a concise overview of linguistic description in the field of English for Academic Purposes, charting its evolution and categorizing the various strands of research interest. Given the increasing use of English as a lingua franca, there has been a corresponding upsurge into research in EAP. The book synthesizes this research in one single volume and offers brief overviews of key terms and topics in EAP, including academic events and study genres, professional research genres and disciplinary discourses. This volume is key reading for graduate students new to the field as well as established researchers looking to expand their knowledge base in EAP. The work highlights the kinds of descriptions of academic English that have resulted from the research, which can be of interest to disciplinary teachers and lecturers, including those in English medium instruction.

Helen Basturkmen is Associate Professor in Applied Linguistics and Language Teaching at the University of Auckland, New Zealand, where she works in research, research supervision and teaching in the Master of Teaching English to Speakers of Other Languages (MTESOL) programme. She edited *English for Academic Purposes* in the *Critical Concepts in Linguistics* Series (2015). Prior to this, she taught English to Speakers of Other Languages (ESOL) and was a teacher educator in the Middle East for many years.

Linguistic Description in English for Academic Purposes

Helen Basturkmen

NEW YORK AND LONDON

First published 2021
by Routledge
605 Third Avenue, New York, NY 10158

and by Routledge
2 Park Square, Milton Park, Abingdon, Oxon OX14 4RN

Routledge is an imprint of the Taylor & Francis Group, an informa business

© 2021 Taylor & Francis

The right of Helen Basturkmen to be identified as author of this work has been asserted by her in accordance with sections 77 and 78 of the Copyright, Designs and Patents Act 1988.

All rights reserved. No part of this book may be reprinted or reproduced or utilised in any form or by any electronic, mechanical, or other means, now known or hereafter invented, including photocopying and recording, or in any information storage or retrieval system, without permission in writing from the publishers.

Trademark notice: Product or corporate names may be trademarks or registered trademarks, and are used only for identification and explanation without intent to infringe.

Library of Congress Cataloging-in-Publication Data
Names: Basturkmen, Helen, author.
Title: Linguistic description in English for academic purposes / Helen Basturkmen.
Description: New York, NY : Routledge, 2021. |
Series: Routledge focus on linguistics |
Includes bibliographical references and index.
Identifiers: LCCN 2021006095 | ISBN 9780815395799 (hardback) |
ISBN 9781351183185 (ebook)
Subjects: LCSH: English language–Study and teaching (Higher)–Foreign speakers. |
English language–Study and teaching (Higher) |
Academic writing–Study and teaching (Higher)
Classification: LCC PE1128.A2 B318 2021 | DDC 428.0071/1–dc23
LC record available at https://lccn.loc.gov/2021006095

ISBN: 978-0-8153-9579-9 (hbk)
ISBN: 978-1-032-00865-3 (pbk)
ISBN: 978-1-351-18318-5 (ebk)

Typeset in Times New Roman
by Newgen Publishing UK

Contents

List of Figures   vii
List of Tables   viii

1   The Expanding Terrain of EAP   1
     1.1 Introduction 1
     1.2 Historical Antecedents and Growing Importance 3
     1.3 Definition of EAP and Scope of the Book 5
     1.4 Contexts 7
     1.5 Summary and Overview of the Book 9

2   Theory and Methodology   14
     2.1 Introduction 14
     2.2 Views of Language and Language Learning 15
     2.3 Discourse Analysis: The Fundamental Methodological Approach 21
     2.4 Variable Methodological Options 25
     2.5 Making Tacitly-held Knowledge Explicit 28

3   The General Academic English Register   33
     3.1 Introduction 33
     3.2 Importance of Description 34
     3.3 The Nature of Description 35
     3.4 Studies in Focus 36

4   Study Genres and Events   46
     4.1 Introduction 46
     4.2 Importance of Description 47
     4.3 Nature of Description 49
     4.4 Studies in Focus 52

5 Professional Research Genres and Events   62
   5.1 Introduction 62
   5.2 Importance 63
   5.3 Nature of Inquiry 65
   5.4 Studies in Focus 68

6 Disciplinary Variation   78
   6.1 Introduction 78
   6.2 Importance of Inquiry 79
   6.3 Nature of Inquiry 83
   6.4 Studies in Focus 85

7 Conclusion and Future Directions   93
   7.1 Introduction 93
   7.2 Directions for Future Empirical Inquiry 93
   7.3 A Classification Framework 96
   7.4 Final comments 98

Index   101

Figures

1.1	Strands of EAP	6
2.1	Traditional pathway for learning academic English	19
2.2	Common core and disciplinary English	19
2.3	Traditional linguistic analysis and discourse analysis	22
2.4	Orientations in discourse analysis	24
2.5	Forms of inquiry	29
3.1	The categories of hedges and evaluation in the AFL. Source: Based on Simpson-Vlach and Ellis (2010: 500–501)	43
4.1	Lecture functions and subfunctions. Source: Based on Deroey & Taverniers (2011: 5)	56
4.2	Interaction patterns in tutorial discussion. Source: Based on Basturkmen (2000; 2003)	58
5.1	Rhetorical moves in TESOL conference proposals. Source: Halleck & Connor, 2006: 73	70
5.2	Moves in RA introductions. Source: Based on Swales (1990: 141)	73
6.1	Classification of interactive and interactional meta discourse. Source: Based on Hyland & Jiang (2018: 20)	87

Tables

1.1	English learning needs and relevance of descriptions	10
2.1	Context, vocabulary and grammar in biology lectures	25
3.1	Grammatical compression structures and implicit meanings	38
3.2	Features associated with informal expression in human interaction and grammatical intricacy categories	40
3.3	Level 1 (most frequent) word families in the Academic Word List	42
3.4	Selection of idioms in academic speaking	44
4.1	Study genres and events	47
4.2	Questions for research and teaching	49
4.3	Selection of recent literature on study genres and events	50
4.4	Social functions of genres of assessed student writing	53
4.5	Six Essay genres with stages	54
5.1	Most prominent classes of patterns in presentations vs. discussion sessions in the JSCC	71
5.2	Patterns used to initialize and react to criticism in the discussion sections of the JSCC	72
6.1	Moves more or less likely to occur in three-minute thesis presentations by disciplinary groupings	86
6.2	Most frequent adjective-noun phrases	89
7.1	A *classification framework for inquiry and description of academic English*	97

1 The Expanding Terrain of EAP

1.1 Introduction

Language description is widely acknowledged as the main intellectual focus of English for Academic Purposes (EAP) (Flowerdew & Peacock, 2001). A substantial body of description of the linguistic features of academic English, which has resulted from over fifty years of research inquiry in the field of EAP, is currently available. This chapter identifies the different groups of readers who may find the work of interest, and it provides background information on the topic of EAP linguistic description – background information about the emergence of EAP as a distinctive branch of English language teaching (ELT) and language description as a major focus of research in it. Although EAP language teaching largely fuelled the initial drive for linguistic descriptions of academic English and prompted much of the research that will be reported in subsequent chapters of this volume, the language description that has resulted from this research has relevance well beyond EAP teaching. It has relevance more broadly to education in general, not only language education.

To date, most EAP linguistic descriptions have been available in ELT and Applied Linguistics journals, such as the *Journal of English for Academic Purposes*, *English for Specific Purposes* and *Applied Linguistics*, and in book chapters in specialist volumes, such as the *Routledge Handbook of English for Academic Purposes* (Hyland & Shaw, 2016) and *Discipline-Specific Writing: Theory into Practice* (Flowerdew & Costley, 2017). The present work aims to provide an overview and synthesis of research in EAP linguistic enquiry in one book and provides background information on the topic of EAP linguistic description.

There is a broad market for the kind of linguistic descriptions of academic English described in the present work. Such descriptions are of obvious relevance to EAP teachers and materials developers, who need to devise teaching materials and activities to highlight the kinds of linguistic forms and patterns involved in academic writing and speaking (Basturkmen, 2019). Although EAP teachers already will be aware of the usefulness of EAP linguistic descriptions for their teaching, they may be seeking a synopsis and overview of research into linguistic description rather than the kind of individual research reports on specific topics that have been available. Busy EAP teachers, who may not have the time or facilities to trawl through the literature, or who do not have access to research journals and specialist books, may welcome a single volume that provides an overview of research and illustrates the kinds of descriptions available in the research literature.

EAP researchers may find the work of interest. They may wish to broaden their knowledge base and find out about different kinds of research and linguistic descriptions. Within the wider field of Applied Linguistics/Language Teaching, researchers in specialisms, such as Second Language Acquisition (SLA), curriculum studies or second-language writing pedagogy, may not be fully aware of the major advances made in EAP and the kinds of descriptions of academic English that have extended knowledge of academic English over recent decades.

The book also targets readers in non-EAP teaching and research contexts, such as teachers of disciplinary subjects in higher education or secondary school. They not only teach disciplinary content – that is, the concepts and ways of thinking and processing information in their subjects – but they also model and highlight how this disciplinary content is expressed linguistically. The language that is used to convey disciplinary content is thus intrinsic to their teaching endeavours. These readers may not be aware of the considerable body of description about academic English and the understanding of disciplinary discourses that have been brought into being by EAP linguistic inquiry. Those researching the development of student or professional academic writing in the fields of education or disciplinary communication may not be familiar with the topics and forms of linguistic inquiry in the EAP literature. Description of research genres, such as research articles, are relevant to the professional interests of nearly all faculty and researchers, regardless of discipline. Similarly, information about the kinds of research conducted to describe language in instructional genres, such as lectures or seminars, would be of interest to those who teach.

It is envisaged that the book will be of relevance also to teachers and lecturers in English Medium Instruction (EMI), a rapidly expanding, global phenomenon (Macaro, 2018; Macaro et al., 2019). In EMI settings around the world, academic subjects, such as biology or economics, are taught in the medium of English rather than in the national, or first language, of the students. Teachers and lecturers in EMI contexts may wish to develop their understanding of the kinds of descriptions of academic English that have become available in EAP. See section 1.4 below for further discussion of contexts for which descriptions of academic English are relevant, including EMI.

The remainder of this chapter examines the terrain of EAP in terms of its historical antecedents and its current position as a world-wide teaching and research endeavour. It provides a definition of EAP, introduces the various strands of EAP and details the contexts for which descriptions of academic English can be of interest.

1.2 Historical Antecedents and Growing Importance

EAP developed out of English for Specific Purposes (ESP), a specialism of English Language Teaching (ELT), and a number of the works cited in this book refer to EAP as part of ESP. ESP had no obvious and incontestable point of origin (Swales, 1985) but rather emerged during the 1960s and early 1970s (Bell, 2016; Dudley-Evans & St John, 1998). EAP materialised as a distinct sub-specialism of ESP when greater numbers of non-English first language background students began studying in universities in English-speaking countries. In the UK, the beginnings of EAP can be traced back to the 1960s when universities began to provide support in the form of short-duration pre-sessional (pre-university) courses and diagnostic language assessments to identify overseas students who might need help (Jordan, 2002). In 1972, SELMOUS, the Special English Language Materials for Overseas University Students organisation, was formed by teachers to support each other in providing materials for the teaching of overseas students. Histories of the early development of EAP in the UK (Bell, 2016; Jordan, 2002; de Chazal, 2014) track the development of EAP largely as a teaching-focused endeavour. However, research came onto the scene when some pioneering EAP teachers began to turn their attention in part to research, usually with the aim of developing descriptions of academic English to draw on and inform the development of their EAP teaching and materials. Clearly, if teachers were going to teach academic English, they needed descriptions of academic English on which to draw.

Although EAP initially grew out the work of teachers in supporting non-native speakers of English with the demands of university studies in English, it is questionable whether EAP as a field of language teaching and linguistic research should continue to be characterised as limited to the needs and interests of non-native speakers of English.

I would argue that EAP has grown into a field that has teaching and research interests of relevance to native and non-native speakers of English. Anyone, regardless of first language, can encounter difficulties understanding or producing academic English. Findings from research into academic English are relevant for all students regardless of first language background (Hewings, Lillis & Mayor, 2007). Studies of research articles or student essays are of interest to English L1 and L2 speakers alike.

The development of EAP teaching and research to provide the kinds of linguistic description described above has continued over five decades. It has been spurred on by the increasing numbers of international students, but also by the adoption of English-medium instruction in certain countries around the world. By 2020, EAP has become an expansive terrain of teaching and research. Why has EAP risen to such prominence? One reason relates to the transformation of universities from essentially national institutions to global institutions that must compete for students and funding, a move that has resulted in a significant increase in the number of international students studying in English-speaking countries, such as the UK, United States, New Zealand and Australia. The student body has become increasingly mobile, and it is no longer only the very few who might travel abroad for their studies.

Numbers of universities around the world have adopted English medium instruction (EMI). For example, some universities in Turkey and Spain provide complete programmes of study, or selected courses, in the medium of English, although most students and faculty are not native speakers of English. Institutions that can provide English medium instruction can attract students from diverse first-language backgrounds and countries of origin. For parents in non-English dominant countries, an English medium education can be viewed as being an important means by which their children will develop the English language skills to open doors upon graduation and offer additional work-related opportunities. For researchers in nearly all disciplines, English has become a requisite academic lingua franca. Increasingly, researchers, regardless of first-language background, vie to get their research published in top-tier English language journals and compete to present their research at major international conferences, which are very often conducted through English. For researchers with a first language other than English, these English-language publications and presentations often hold much importance when the researchers attempt to advance their careers and seek promotions or tenure. The impetus for academics to publish in high ranking journals has led to an "explosion" of articles and books as academics compete for research outputs to meet the demands of "unforgiving and numerically driven" university research assessment schemes (Hyland, 2015: 22).

On a personal note, I began teaching English as a foreign language in Turkey in the late 1970s. At that time, only relatively few English language teachers were teaching EAP, even in university contexts. Three and a half decades later, this situation has changed considerably. Many now teach in English preparatory programmes targeting new entrants to the universities, or on language courses provided to students already in university programmes delivered through English. Turkey can best be regarded as a country in which English in the wider community, that is beyond higher education, is a foreign language. Yet, according to an official publication, out of Turkey's 20 top-ranking universities, 6 have English as the medium of instruction, 4 have Turkish and 12 have a mix of English and Turkish-medium instruction (TEPAV, 2015).

In New Zealand, an English-speaking country where I currently work, universities and other institutions of higher education have a long tradition of attracting international students. The official languages of New Zealand are English, Maori and New Zealand Sign Language. Over time, EAP courses in New Zealand higher education have increased in range, and now include pre-sessional courses for international students, general academic writing courses catering for English L1 and L2 students, disciplinary writing courses for students already enrolled in their departments and courses on academic writing and presenting for graduate students. A few years ago, I was a visiting academic at a university in the south of Spain. In that setting, many English-language teachers had become involved in teaching and developing EAP courses and materials (Bocanegra-Valle & Basturkmen, 2019) and some in teaching English to faculty for research publication purposes. EMI had been adopted in principle in that university, although its implementation varied according to departments and courses.

1.3 Definition of EAP and Scope of the Book

The following definition of EAP is proposed:

> EAP is a theoretically and empirically based field of inquiry that aims to identify the linguistic features of academic English and the forms and patterning of English academic texts and talk, to understand how academic English can be taught and how it is acquired, in both instructed and naturalistic, disciplinary contexts, including English medium instruction.

This definition, which is based on a definition of ESP in Basturkmen (2020), is broader than most earlier definitions, which tend to define EAP in quite narrow terms as the teaching of English language and communication skills necessary for study in higher education (Bell, 2016). The definition I propose above encompasses EAP teaching and learning (and research into teaching and learning) as well linguistic inquiry to identify and describe academic English. The focus of the present work, however, is limited to linguistic inquiry – inquiry that aims to identify the linguistic features of academic English and the forms and patterning of English academic texts and talk – and the kinds of descriptions of academic English that have resulted from it. It is beyond the scope of the work to examine teaching and learning, or research into teaching and learning of academic English.

The present work includes research motivated by two different strands of interest. The first, English for Study Purposes, concerns the texts and talk students encounter. The second, English for Professional Academic Purposes, is concerned with texts and talk in genres, such as research articles and conference proposals, which are important for professional academics (see Figure 1.1).

The terms English for General Academic Purposes (EGAP) and English for Specific Academic Purposes (ESAP) are widely used in the EAP literature. EGAP refers to the uses of academic English without reference to specific academic disciplines. Teaching or research in this area tends to focus on what is seen as a common core of academic

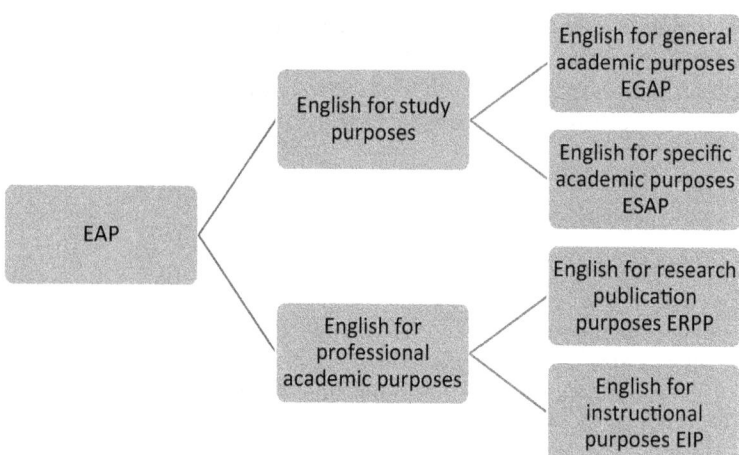

Figure 1.1 Strands of EAP.

English-language structures, vocabulary and text types. These are general in the sense that they occur across disciplines (see Chapter 2 for a critical discussion of this perspective). ESAP refers to the uses of English in specific disciplines or disciplinary settings, such as English for economics or English for social studies. Inter alia, ESAP teaching and research focuses on disciplinary vocabulary, writing conventions, and disciplinary genre practices.

Currently, most published research into academic English and EAP teaching concerns tertiary education. This may reflect the original emergence of EAP in response to the difficulties and needs of international university students (Bell, 2016). There has been limited research in EAP concerning the academic language needs, skills and texts used in school settings, although it is widely acknowledged that students encounter, and are required to produce, academic English well in advance of university study. Most of the descriptions of academic English examined in the present work are based on research into texts and talk in higher education or research settings. However, where possible, I have included references to EAP research in school settings.

1.4 Contexts

Descriptions of academic and disciplinary English are relevant to the interests of different groups. Contexts vary greatly. In some educational settings, English is used as the primary or only language for instruction. In others, it is used partially. For example, Pecorari, Shaw, Malmström and Irvine (2011) describe the use of English textbooks in Swedish universities, a setting in which education is generally through the national language. English language textbooks and other reading materials were once sometimes used due to the unavailability of quality materials in the national language (the markets for textbooks published in English is generally greater, and publishers are able to provide more funds for textbook development). Now, however, English language textbooks are often selected, not because of a lack of an alternative, but because of the possibility that incidental English learning will result from reading, which may help the students with their future career needs.

Descriptions of disciplinary discourses (how English is used in a discipline, such as history or biology) have a wide potential reach. The initial years of disciplinary study introduce students to not only disciplinary content but also expose them to the linguistic register of the discipline, including its specialised vocabulary. This register is often relatively new for English L1 background and English L2 background students alike. Clearly, descriptions of disciplinary discourses are of key interest to all those working within a discipline, including researchers, lecturers and students.

Descriptions of disciplinary discourses are relevant to the interests of those in EMI settings around the world. Recent years have witnessed the rapid growth of EMI, an approach to teaching disciplinary content subjects, such as science, economics, or political science, using English. Unlike EAP teaching, which targets English-language learning outcomes, EMI targets content-learning outcomes, and English is generally referred to simply as the language in which the course is taught (Airey, 2016). Mostly, EMI has been adopted in higher-education settings. However, EMI is becoming increasingly common at elementary and secondary education levels. In South Korea, EMI has become well established in higher education and some secondary schools, both public and private, have begun to adopt EMI (Hong & Basturkmen, 2020).

Some scholars use the term EMI to refer only to teaching academic subjects in English where the general population has a first language other than English (Macaro, 2018). However, in some English-speaking contexts, such as New Zealand or the UK, both the student body and faculty have become increasingly international in composition, with members coming from diverse first-language backgrounds. Here the distinction between English-dominant and non-dominant settings is blurred. The distinction thus seems of limited relevance to the topic of the present work (language description). It is, however, relevant to other EMI-related topics, such as language policy at national or institutional levels (Dearden, 2015; Kirkpatrick & Liddicoat, 2017; Macaro et al., 2018).

General academic and disciplinary English are learnt registers. They are no one's mother tongue, and they are generally acquired later in life. Students and faculty in many contexts in which disciplinary-content subjects are taught using English may wish to draw on descriptions of general academic and disciplinary English, as they are involved in developing these registers or helping others develop these registers. Green and Lambert (2019) highlight the increasing specialisation of study in school education, saying that from around middle school texts become technical and specialised and thus benefit from a disciplinary approach, and core disciplinary ideas are set out in secondary-school life. In the secondary-school sector, "disciplinary literacy" is a term more commonly used than are the terms "English for specific academic purposes" or "learning disciplinary discourses," which are more widely used in Applied Linguistics and EAP. Acquiring "disciplinary literacy" can be described as learning to read, think, communicate and use information in a way similar to that of discipline experts (Green & Lambert, 2019: 2). In secondary school and university contexts, it is not a general English proficiency that is being developed but rather the development of academic English and disciplinary varieties (depending on which school subjects or university disciplines the student is taking).

There is a growing body of research evidence to suggest that disciplinary teachers and lecturers recognise the intrinsic role of language in teaching and learning content. They do not expect their students to simply learn disciplinary discourse through exposure to talk and texts, nor do they perceive their role as limited – simply modelling this discourse. Investigation of disciplinary classrooms in EMI university contexts, including classes with mixed English L1 and L2 background students (Basturkmen & Shackleford, 2015) has shown that during their teaching disciplinary teachers and lecturers intermittently draw their students' attention to language, often to focus on specialised vocabulary. This has been found also to be the case in secondary-school EMI classrooms in South Korea (Hong & Basturkmen, 2020). Teachers in primary-school settings, too, have been observed to help English L2 learners with the language they need to describe scientific concepts (Gibbons, 2003).

Different groups would likely have interests in and/or need to acquire different academic discourses and genres, as shown in Table 1.1. Research faculty and graduate students would likely be interested in research discourse, descriptions of expert disciplinary writing and speaking and genres, such as research articles and conference presentations. Lecturers and teachers would likely have interests in disciplinary discourses as well as instructional genres, such as lectures. Descriptions of study genres, such as student essays, as well as disciplinary discourses could be of interest to students and to those who support students with their academic writing and academic English development.

1.5 Summary and Overview of the Book

I have argued above that linguistic descriptions of academic English can be of relevance to quite diverse groups in various educational and research settings, not only to EAP teachers. However, the body of knowledge currently available in EAP needs to extend its reach and impact to broader educational and research contexts. For professional academics and disciplinary lecturers and teachers, knowledge about academic English may remain limited to a few ideas gleaned from academic writing style guides or vague notions of the need for academic English to be formal rather than precise knowledge about the choice of language features that distinguish academic writing from

Table 1.1 English learning needs and relevance of descriptions

Group	Focus	Strand of EAP inquiry	Academic English that needs to be acquired	Example communicative events & genres of relevance
Faculty & graduate students	Research discourses	English for publication purposes	Expert disciplinary writing & speaking practices	Research articles Conference proposals & presentations
Faculty, teaching assistants and teachers	Instructional discourses	English for instructional purposes	Monologic & interactive speaking & listening skills	Lectures, seminars & tutorials Labs. Office-hour & supervisory meetings
Students	Student discourses	English for study purposes		
		General academic purposes	Formal academic English register (linguistic features, writing conventions, rhetorical styles & norms) Study skills & competencies	Lectures Lessons Presentations & discussions Textbooks (reading) Essay & assignment writing
		Specific academic purposes	Disciplinary English Writing/speaking practices appropriate for student performance in the discipline(s)	Depending on discipline: e.g. laboratory reports in sciences, case study reports in business studies

the language used in everyday, conversational English. For disciplinary teachers, lecturers and their students, knowledge of academic written texts may remain limited to rather basic ideas about essay structure and paragraph organisation. Yet, much more information about both general academic and disciplinary English is now available and, importantly, this knowledge is based on empirical research. The aim of this volume is to provide an overview of the kinds of EAP linguistic research and the nature of the descriptions that have resulted from it and to showcase this research in order to extend its potential reach and impact.

The interests of EAP have broadened, and it is no longer restricted to teaching or researching a set of generic English study skills. Rather it now includes teaching and research in English for specific academic purposes, research publication purposes and instructional purposes. EAP research has gone far beyond some rather general descriptions of study writing to prepare students for the onset of academic writing in the university context. The range of academic linguistic descriptions that have become available through research conducted in EAP is now much wider as the reader will see in the following chapters.

Chapter 2 examines theory and methodology in EAP linguistic research. It describes major theories in this field, such as genre theory and academic literacies perspectives and methodologies for linguistic analysis, such as corpus analysis and ethnographic enquiry. Chapter 3 focuses on research that has provided descriptions of general academic English. Chapter 4 examines descriptions of English as used for instructional purposes in academic events, such as seminars and lectures, and for study purposes. Chapter 5 brings together research findings from studies that have investigated professional research genres, such as research articles. Research into disciplinary variation is examined in Chapter 6. Chapters 3 to 6 are similarly organised – they describe the aims, importance, and nature of inquiry on the topic before a "Studies in Focus" section that showcases a selection of specific studies and illustrates the kind of description of academic English they have provided. Chapter 7 concludes the book with a discussion of future developments and suggestions for the research agenda.

References

Airey, J. (2016). EAP, EMI or CLIL. In K. Hyland & P. Shaw (Eds), *The Routledge handbook of English for academic purposes* (pp. 71–83). Abingdon, Oxon: Routledge.

Basturkmen, H. (2019). ESP teacher education needs. *Language Teaching*, 52(3): 318–330.
Basturkmen, H. (2020). Is ESP a materials and teaching-led movement? *Language Teaching*, 1–11. doi:10.1017/S0261444820000300
Basturkmen, H., & Shackleford, N. (2015). How content lecturers help students with language: An observational study of language-related episodes in first year accounting classrooms. *English for Specific Purposes*, 37: 87–97.
Bell, D. (2016). *Practitioners, pedagogies and professionalism in English for academic purposes (EAP): The development of a contested field.* (Unpublished PhD dissertation). University of Nottingham, Nottingham.
Bocanegra-Valle, A. & Basturkmen, H. (2019). Investigating the teacher education needs of experienced ESP teachers in Spanish universities. *Ibérica*, 38: 127–149.
De Chazal, E. (2014). *English for academic purposes.* Oxford: Oxford University Press.
Dearden, J. (2015). *English as a medium of instruction: A growing global phenomenon.* Oxford: British Council.
Dudley-Evans, T. & St John, M.J. (1998). *Developments in ESP. A multi-disciplinary approach.* Cambridge: Cambridge University Press.
Flowerdew, J. & Costley, T. (Eds) (2017). *Discipline-specific writing: Theory into practice.* London: Routledge.
Flowerdew, J. & Peacock, M. (2001). Issues in EAP: A preliminary perspective. In J. Flowerdew, & M. Peacock, M. (Eds), *Research perspectives on English for academic purposes* (pp. 8–24). Cambridge: Cambridge University Press.
Gibbons, G. (2003). Mediating language learning: Teacher interactions with ESL students in a content-based classroom. *TESOL Quarterly*, 37: 247–273.
Green, C. & Lambert, J. (2019). Position vectors, homologous chromosomes and gamma rays: Promoting disciplinary literacy through secondary phrase lists. *English for Specific Purposes*, 53: 1–12.
Hewings, A., Lillis, T. & Mayor, B. (2007). Academic writing in English. In N. Mercer, J. Swann & B. Mayor (Eds), *Learning English* (pp. 227–259). Abingdon: Routledge.
Hong, J. & Basturkmen, H. (2020). Incidental attention to academic language during content teaching in two EMI classes in South Korean high schools. *Journal of English for Academic Purposes*, 48.
Hyland, K. (2015). *Academic publishing: Issues and challenges in the construction of knowledge.* Oxford: Oxford University Press.
Hyland, K. & Shaw, P. (2016). *The Routledge handbook of English for academic purposes.* London: Routledge.
Jordan, R.R. (2002). The growth of EAP in Britain. *Journal of English for Academic Purposes*, 1: 69–78.
Kirkpatrick, A., & Liddicoat, A. (2017). Language education policy and practice in East and Southeast Asia. *Language Teaching*, 50(2): 155–188.
Macaro, E. (2018). *English medium instruction: Content and language in policy and practice.* Oxford: Oxford University Press.

Macaro, E., Curle, S., Pun, J., An, J., & Dearden, J. (2018). A systematic review of English medium instruction in higher education. *Language Teaching,* 51(1): 36–76.
Macaro, E., Hultgren, A., Kirkpatrick, A., & Lasagabaster, D. (2019). English medium instruction: Global views and countries in focus. *Language Teaching,* 52(2): 231–248.
Pecorari, D., Shaw, P., Malmström, H., & Irvine, A. (2011). English textbooks in parallel language tertiary education. *Teaching English to Speakers of Other Languages Quarterly*, 45 (2): 313–333.
Swales, J. (1985). *Episodes in ESP: A source and reference book on the development of English for science and technology*. Hemel Hempstead: Prentice Hall.
TEPAV, Türkiye Ekonomi Politikalari Araştirma Vakfi (2015). *The state of English in higher education in Turkey*. Ankara: Yorum Basin Yayin Sanayi.

2 Theory and Methodology

2.1 Introduction

Linguistic inquiry in EAP has very largely sought to provide information about typical uses of English in academic settings. EAP linguistic inquiry has largely been spurred by pedagogic aims to provide language descriptions that can be drawn on in EAP teaching. Broadly speaking, the methodology used to produce these descriptions largely involves observing and analysing texts or samples of academic and disciplinary English produced by successful professional or student writers and speakers (see discussion of discourse analysis below). Countless studies have drawn, for their data, on published research articles, usually in journals that involve a rigorous peer review process. To be published, the articles have met disciplinary expectations for the content of the research but also for their linguistic quality in terms of written expression, style and organisation, Similarly, descriptions of study writing draw on samples of successful student writing for data (Nesi & Gardner, 2012).

This chapter examines the nature of EAP linguistic inquiry and provides background information on theory and research methodology. Key concepts, including discourse, register, discourse communities and disciplinary English, are introduced. The chapter discusses the changing perspectives on learning and teaching academic English that have fuelled developments in linguistic inquiry. Discourse analysis is proposed as the fundamental methodology used in inquiry, and the chapter details the characteristic uses of discourse analysis drawn on to build descriptions of academic English. Further methodological options, including the use of corpus analysis and ethnographic techniques, are introduced. The chapter concludes with a discussion of the role of EAP linguistic inquiry in making explicit the generally tacitly held knowledge of academic discourse communities and disciplines.

2.2 Views of Language and Language Learning

Cohen and Manion argue (1980: 15) that, although a theory may present a unified view of phenomena, in reality it is often a convenient way of organising multifarious facts and ideas "to make sense out of what we know." I would argue that a social view of language underpins most linguistic inquiry in the field of EAP. This view should be seen in the sense described by Cohen and Manion, that is, as a post-event rationalisation rather than as an a priori theory.

Language is seen as a means of communication used by academics, teachers and students to achieve their goals in the academy and in their disciplines. Broadly speaking, EAP linguistic inquiry has not adhered to a mentalist view of language in which English is seen as an abstract code, and inquiry has not investigated language as a form of internalised cognition. Rather, it has investigated how language is used in practice in academic settings and in disciplinary communities as the means of getting things done.

As in ELT in general, EAP has been influenced by the linguistic anthropologist and sociolinguist, Dell Hymes, and the notion of communicative competence. Hymes (1987) argued that the object of linguistic inquiry should be communicative competence, which comprised not just linguistic competence (knowing the grammar, or the linguistic system) but also social competence (knowing what is appropriate in terms of linguistic behaviour, and knowing what is really done in language), as determined through observing real language use. The dominant trend at the time was for inquiry to have linguistic competence, which was typically seen as sentence-level grammar, as the object of inquiry. The communicative competence view suggested a more extensive focus on language and a shift away from the view that language was "the internalised knowledge of the rules" of a language (Jaworski & Coupland, 2014: 21), in which rules were primarily seen as the rules of grammar. The sentence was no longer the object of inquiry but rather a community's conventionalised patterns of communication and typical language choices in language-based events. Key ideas that have come to characterise EAP linguistic inquiry that relate to the notion of communicative competence include:

- The aim of providing description of language-based, academic events (rather than sentence grammar)
- The use of observation (rather than introspection)
- The focus on routine, conventional patterns of language use as evidence of language that is appropriate and language practices in the academy or in disciplines

The work of John Swales is widely recognised as the most important contribution to EAP linguistic description and theory to date. Swales stressed the social nature of language through the concept of discourse communities. A discourse community was defined in the following terms:

> A discourse community has a broadly agreed set of common public goals, mechanisms of intercommunication among its members, uses its participatory mechanisms primarily to provide information and feedback, utilises and hence possesses one or more genres in the communicative furtherance of its aims. In addition to owning genres, a discourse community has acquired some specific lexis and has a threshold level of members with a suitable degree of relevant content and discoursal expertise.
>
> (Swales, 1990: 24–27)

Discourse communities can be academic or non-academic. Members of a discipline are an example of an academic discourse community. They share the goal of advancing knowledge in their field, and they have mechanisms of participation (conferences and journals) and genres (conference proposals and journal articles) that they use on a regular basis. A community can be local, national or international – for example, the University of Auckland Marine Biology Group, New Zealand Marine Biologists, or the International Association of Marine Biologists. Members need knowledge of marine biology and the ability to engage with the discipline's discourse.

Swales's conceptualisation of genres and the approach to genre analysis he developed have been highly influential. Swales (1990) defined genre as a category of communicative event, examples of which have a common set of communicative purposes. Examples of a genre, as well as purpose, have commonalities in organisational patterns of structure, content, linguistic style and intended audience. A plethora of EAP linguistic studies have drawn on this construct to investigate and describe the typical organisational pattern (content and sequence) of particular academic genres, especially written genres. EAP linguistic inquiry can target different levels of specificity. Swales (2019) provides the following illustration and points out that most EAP research focuses on levels 4–7, although EAP teaching might focus on any level including level 1, and level 8 if teaching subject specialists, such as postdoc students.

1. Academic writing
2. Research writing

3. Research papers
4. Empirical research papers
5. Quantitative empirical research papers
6. Quantitative empirical research papers in sociology
7. Quantitative empirical research papers in the sociology of medicine
8. Quantitative empirical research papers published in the *Sociology of Medicine*

(Swales, 2019: 75)

Ken Hyland, a second major contributor to EAP linguistic description and theory, highlights the relationship between discourse communities and the features of text (discourse). Hyland's work positions disciplines as central to an understanding of academic discourse.

> Language is not just a means for self-expression then, it is how we construct and sustain reality, and we do this as members of communities, using the language of those communities. The features of a text are therefore influenced by the community for which it was written and so best understood, and taught, through the specific genres of communities.

(Hyland, 2002: 41)

The relationship between discourse and disciplines has long been a topic of interest to scholars in the field of education. It has been recognised that as disciplines evolve, they develop their own language conventions and practices. Certain expressions and patterns of organisation become conventionalised over time, and new words are created to refer to newly discovered or specially defined objects or processes. For example, Applied Linguists have words such as *willingness to communicate*, *uptake*, *acquisition*, and *genre awareness*. Other less obvious conventions include criteria for what is relevant content and appropriate forms of argument (Wells, 1992).

2.2.1 Views of Learning Academic English

The Learning Pathway

This section examines two views of learning academic English, views of the learning pathway and views of the targets of learning.

Do Learners Need Basic English before They Can Learn Academic English?

One commonly held view is that academic English is a variety of English rooted in and extending from a common core of general or basic English. The common core includes the grammar system and high-frequency vocabulary that is general to all areas of use, that is, language that is commonly drawn on in all kinds of areas and situations. The common core is seen as a pool of linguistic forms that dominates all varieties of English. It is usual practice for learners of English to be required to take a general English course to gain the common core as a prerequisite for entry to an academic English course or to achieve a certain level of general English before being allowed entry to an academic English course (academic English is seen as one variety of English).

However, the idea of a common core, and that learners need to acquire it before academic English is a taken-for-granted assumption rather than a topic that has been subject to theoretical and empirical research. Theoretically, the common core is a linguistic abstraction. Language is used everywhere and always for a purpose, and the meaning it carries depends on the context not only on the grammatical features and the root meaning of words included (lexical items). To illustrate, "It is going to rain" in the context of a meteorology report may "mean" a future event of water falling from the sky. In a context of a discussion by airline pilots, the utterance could be used to warn of a potential problem.

An alternative view is that English only exists in one variety or another, such as medical English, academic English or casual conversational English. The "core" does not exist in advance of a variety but rather it is where varieties overlap. There is no basic, variety-less English, or no general English. As the language only exists as one variety or another, learning a general English (the common core) does not need to take place before learning a variety, such as academic English. Learners of academic English would be better off learning "the basics" from academic English because exposure to academic texts is more likely to provide appropriate form-meaning correlates (Bloor & Bloor, 1986):

> All language learning is acquired from one variety or another, even if it is "classroom English" variety. A language learner is as likely to acquire "the language" from one variety as from another, but the use of language, being geared to situation and participants, is learned in appropriate contexts.
>
> (Bloor & Bloor, 1986: 28)

Do Learners Need General Academic English before They Can Learn Disciplinary English?

Conventionally, learners take EGAP (general academic English) courses before progressing to ESAP (a course in disciplinary English; see Figure 2.1). General academic English courses are very much in evidence around the world, often in the initial year of university study or in pre-sessional programs. Course content might include study skills, such as listening and note-taking, linguistic features of "academic style," such as hedging, and essay writing, skills and genres that are thought to be relevant across the different disciplines the students will study. This kind of course is sometimes referred to as "wide-angled" (Basturkmen, 2015). After this, learners may progress to an ESAP course, if one is available. The ESAP course might focus on disciplinary genres, expectations for student writing in essays and other forms of assessed writing in the discipline, support for reading disciplinary texts and developing disciplinary vocabulary.

General academic English, like the common core, is an abstraction. All uses of academic English come from one discipline or another, although there are overlaps where the varieties draw on the same linguistic pool (see Figure 2.2). The learners' goal is generally to be able

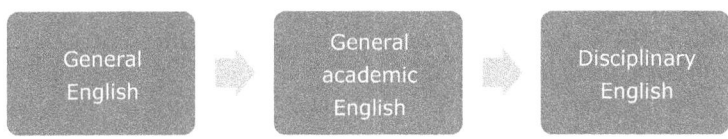

Figure 2.1 Traditional pathway for learning academic English.

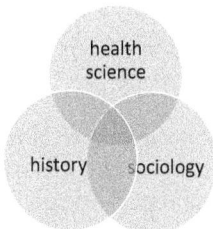

Figure 2.2 Common core and disciplinary English.

to use English well in their disciplinary study. Should learners be able to bypass general academic English courses and go directly to ESAP? This may be possible depending on how much language support the learner needs or how much support the ESAP teacher could provide. However, although general academic English is a pseudo variety (an abstraction) EGAP courses provide an important, supportive foundation for study in the medium of English. The widespread emergence and continued use of EGAP courses around the world would seem to attest to their value.

2.2.2 Targets of Learning

Four stages have been evident in the history of EAP teaching (Hyland, 2006). Each was premised on a different view of the target of learning and led to a distinct teaching/learning approach. (For a review of the history of linguistic research in EAP, see Swales, 2001.) The approaches have reflected and fuelled developments in EAP linguistic inquiry. The earliest stage was based on a view that the target of learning was the acquisition of the grammatical and lexical properties of scientific and technical texts. At that time, most international students in UK and US universities were studying these fields. This situation served as impetus for work such as *The Structure of Technical English* (Herbert, 1965).

The second stage viewed the object of learning as a set of generic skills for study purposes. The study-skills approach emerged in the 1970s and is still in evidence in some settings. The focus is on developing learners' linguistic skills, namely academic reading, writing, speaking and listening, and the micro skills (specific components) of these skills. For example, academic-listening micro skills include listening for topic shifts in lectures and listening and note-taking. In "listening for topic shifts in lectures," listeners need to pay attention to the typical linguistic realisations, such as *turning now to, next I will look at*, used in lectures. Linguistic inquiries were needed to provide description of typical linguistic realisations. The study skills approach underpins many EGAP courses. The skills are thought to be common across disciplines, thus constituting a kind of common core of study skills (Basturkmen, 2015).

Two further stages, which concern teaching academic writing, are current today. The disciplinary socialisation approach era emerged in the wake of work by Swales (1990). In this approach, learning academic writing is seen not as acquisition of generic academic skills but as a form of acculturation into a disciplinary discourse community, with teaching providing descriptions of disciplinary practice of study genres, such as argumentative essays in philosophy or case-study reports in business studies, so that learners can come to "reproduce particular discourse forms" that are acceptable to their lecturers and professors (Hyland, 2006: 21). Novice academics, too, need to learn how to reproduce specific discourse forms, such as disciplinary research articles and meet expectations of their wider disciplinary community. This target of learning draws on and fuels much of the EAP inquiry into disciplinary communication, especially written genres.

The academic-literacies approach aims to help learners understand and critique the complex and highly specific nature of discursive practices in their fields and across subjects in their fields. Like the socialisation approach, the target of learning in the academic-literacies approach is discourse practices in specific contexts. However, this approach focuses not only on genres that are specific to disciplines but even to different subject areas within a disciplinary area. Students are helped to "engage in, understand and critique the discursive practices" of these contexts (Hyland, 2006: 223). This orientation serves as an impetus for, and a reflection of, inquiry into disciplinary variation.

2.3 Discourse Analysis: The Fundamental Methodological Approach

2.3.1 Discourse and Texts

Linguistic description has been the central concern of EAP to date. Nearly all studies have used discourse analysis, where the object of inquiry is "actual instances of communicative action in the medium of language" (Johnstone, 2008: 2), typically of texts. Discourse is a stretch, or spate, of language use. Researchers have sought to understand and provide descriptions of the overall functions or goals of the texts and their structure and the typical linguistic choices made by writers and speakers in them. The texts can be written, such as essays or research articles, or spoken, such as lectures and seminars or research presentations.

Texts are units of language used for communicative purposes, such as to report research (a research report text or genre) or to argue the need for a research study (a rationale or justification section in a research article or in a research grant application). Texts derive their meaning primarily from their situated use. In other words, we can only understand the meanings expressed in the texts by considering the overall function the texts have in their contexts of use. Although texts can be any length (even a one-word message, such as an "Exit" sign in a cinema, can be considered to be a text as it is a complete unit of communication), most academic texts are long and complex and from this it follows that texts are structured and made up of sub units. One focus of EAP linguistic research is to identify how complex texts are typically structured. The texts examined in this research are authentic, that is, they are naturally occurring data. They are texts that were produced by students, academics and researchers to meet their study, research or teaching goals in academic and research settings. They were not fabricated for the purposes of linguistic analysis.

For some readers, the term *linguistic analysis* may be redolent of the kind of sentence-level grammar analysis that they experienced in learning languages and using traditional grammar books in school. However, discourse analysis is different from traditional linguistic analysis which tended to focus on sentence level grammar without context, and meaning was seen as derived from the syntactic, morphological and lexical components of the sentence. See Figure 2.3. Traditional linguistic analysis was concerned with the formal properties of language, typically with sentence construction in invented or idealised language samples. Discourse analysis is by contrast a descriptive approach to linguistic description. It examines stretches of language use in context. Meanings are understood to emanate from linguistic components in relation to the purposes of the text (situated uses of language). In other words, meanings are not considered to reside in the syntactic, morphological or lexical components alone. Unlike traditional linguistic analysis which often used fabricated language samples as data for analysis or for exemplification, discourse analysis is based on observation of naturally

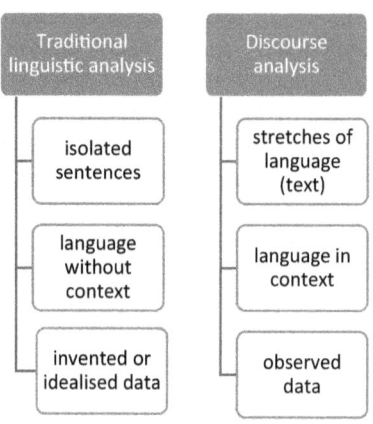

Figure 2.3 Traditional linguistic analysis and discourse analysis.

occurring language samples, which are usually texts. Johnstone explains that the term *discourse analysis* rather than *language analysis* highlights that the focus is not on language as an abstract system but rather on what happens when people use language "to do things in the world" (Johnstone, 2008: 3).

2.3.2 Orientations

Some EAP discourse analyses have had a text linguistic orientation. A text linguistic type inquiry aims to identify language patterns or structures beyond clause or sentence level. This is similar to traditional linguistic analysis in that it is a search for the formal properties of language (context-free regularities), and discourse may even be seen as a kind of extra-long sentence (Hopper, 1987). However, unlike some traditional linguistic analysis, a textlinguistic discourse approach examines naturally occurring samples of language use.

Studies with a discourse and society orientation are concerned with the relationship between speakers/writers and the discourse they produce, with the aim of understanding language use of specific discourse communities, such as a particular discipline or the academic community at large. Discourse analysis with this orientation aims to develop an understanding of what language choices people in a community or discipline typically make and what they mean by their choices.

"Discourse analysis also looks at social and cultural settings of language use to help us understand how it is that people come to make particular choices in their use of language" (Paltridge & Wang, 2010: 256). The aims of these different orientations to discourse analysis are shown in Figure 2.4.

Text linguistic and discourse and society orientation type studies have descriptive goals. One further orientation is critical discourse analysis. This orientation has links with the discourse and society orientation, but critical theorists draw on discourse analysis to pursue critical goals.

> The terms "discourse" and "discourse analysis" have different meanings to scholars in different fields. For many, particularly linguistics, "discourse" has generally been defined as anything "beyond the sentence." For others, the study of discourse is the study of language use. These definitions have in common a focus on specific instances or spates of language. But critical theorists and those influenced by them can speak, for example, of "discourse of power" and "discourse of racism," where the term "discourses"

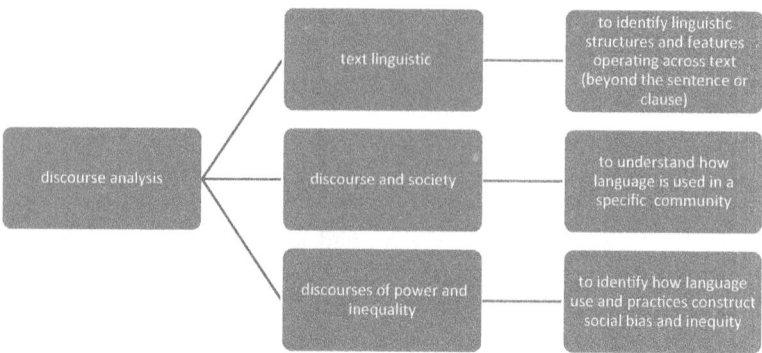

Figure 2.4 Orientations in discourse analysis.

not only becomes a count noun, but further refers to a broad conglomeration of linguistic and non-linguistic social practices and ideological assumptions that together construct power and racism.
(Schriffin, Tannen & Hamilton, 2001: 1)

The following chapters examine studies of discourse with descriptive goals, that is inquiry that aims "to describe the world or whatever bit of the world the researcher is interested in" (Johnstone, 2008: 27). In EAP research that "bit of the world" is English in academic and research settings. Johnston identifies two general assumptions underlying discourse analysis with descriptive goals: (1) that it is possible to describe the world and that there is not a limitless number of possible descriptions; and (2) that the role of the researcher is to describe the "status quo" (Johnstone, 2008: 27).

2.3.3 Academic Registers, Events and Genres – Objects of Discourse Inquiry

EAP linguistic inquiries have investigated registers, events and genres. The terms *variety* and *register* are used interchangeably in the present work. The term register (or variety) is the "language associated with a field or profession" (Flowerdew, 2013: 138), or a "functional language variation" (Swales, 1990: 40). The object of inquiry can be the general academic register, such as academic English, or a specific register, such as medical research English. Lectures, and seminars are types of academic events. Inquiry can focus on an academic event in general

Table 2.1 Context, vocabulary and grammar in biology lectures

Context	Vocabulary and Grammar
The expert lecturer provides information to students about a topic in biology by means of an informal spoken monologue that includes dialogues when questions are asked. The monologue is expository text that is supported with visuals.	Biology vocabulary that includes relational and process verbs. Grammatical structures that include declaratives, and some use of imperatives (e.g. *look at this*) and interrogatives in questions. Some discourse markers to show lecture structure (e.g. *well, right*).

Source: Table 2.1 draws on information in Flowerdew (2013: 14).

(seminars) or in a specific discipline (seminars in business studies). The description of grammar and vocabulary in biology lectures in Table 2.1 illustrates a description of an academic event in a specific discipline. Similarly, inquiry can focus on a genre in general, such as the expository student essay, a widely used study genre, or the practice of a genre in a specific discipline, such as the medical research article abstract, or a discipline-specific genre, such as the *problem question* in law studies (Nesi & Gardner, 2012). One perspective of the relationship between genres and registers reviewed in Swales (1990) proposes that register constraints operate at the linguistic level of vocabulary and syntax, but genre constraints operate at the level of discourse structure. Genres, such as the research report, can only be realised as complete texts, which is not the case for registers, such as the language of scientific reporting. The data used in EAP linguistic inquiry differs depending on the focus. If the inquiry focuses on a genre, complete texts of that genre are needed. Of course, if the inquiry focuses on a part genre, such as the research article abstract, complete samples of the part genre are used as data. If the inquiry focuses on a register, samples of text (not necessarily, complete texts), often including a mix of genres, are used as data.

2.4 Variable Methodological Options

Although the great majority of linguistic inquiries in EAP are similar in having a methodology that is discourse analytical in the sense that they are based on observations of naturally occurring texts (language use) as data, they have varied in terms of whether they involve a quantitative and/or qualitative approach, the use of descriptive or inferential statistics, manual analysis and/or corpus analysis software, and whether they include examination of the contexts in which texts or discourse are used.

In conducting a genre analysis, it is possible to include only qualitative analysis. The researcher might take a target genre – for example, the conclusion sections of research reports – collect a small data set of 15 sample sections and simply seek to describe what moves (stretches of language that serve a specific communicative function) writers can include. However, the researcher might add a quantitative dimension to the study by including some simple frequency counts of how many of the samples included each of the move options. Yet, another researcher working at a later time – when descriptions of the conclusion section have become established in the field and show that the conclusion involves three or four key moves – might adopt an entirely quantitative approach and seek to identify how often each move occurs in two data sets such as research reports in two different disciplines or in texts written by novice or seasoned academic writers. In the latter case, the researcher is likely to collect a far larger set of texts as data. The researcher might also hypothesise that novices could use the moves less consistently than would seasoned writers, or seek to identify whether any moves are used more often by one of the two groups. The purely qualitative inquiry described above can be related to Seliger and Shohamy's description of heuristic research, which they define as follows:

> We proceed from the data, the actual data or unprocessed observations, to patterns which are suggested by the data themselves ... Having a heuristic objective to the research enables us to discover patterns, behaviours, explanations, and to form questions or actual hypotheses for further research.
> (Seliger & Shohamy, 1989: 30)

The inquiries described above that focused on the consistency or frequency of the moves can be related to Seliger and Shohamy's description of "deductive or hypothesis-testing research" that is based on a "preconceived notion" about the phenomenon of interest (Seliger and Shohamy, 1989: 30).

To an extent, these different research objectives relate to the dichotomy between qualitative and quantitative research. Qualitative linguistic research aims to identify a feature or pattern, or to describe its characteristics. Quantitative linguistic research often aims to include a large set of data (samples) so that inferences can be made about any variables at play. It uses either descriptive statistics, such as average scores, frequency counts or percentages, or inferential statistics to investigate the likelihood of a relationship (Phakiti & Paltridge, 2015). Studies discussed in the following chapters have qualitative and quantitative aims, and some studies have both. Although many of the studies with quantitative aims employed descriptive statistics, a limited number of the studies used inferential statistics.

Many EAP linguistic inquiries have drawn on computer software for corpus analysis. Computers enable "consistent and accurate" analysis of large databases and are used for processes, such as identifying the frequency of words or phrases, concordancing (providing lists of given linguistic items within sufficient surrounding text to determine syntactic, semantic, and pragmatic properties) and parsing (syntactic analysis) (Flowerdew, 2013, 3–4). Corpus-based approaches are widely used for building language descriptions of specialised academic writing (Flowerdew, 2017).

Although computer software is employed to quantify the use of a linguistic feature it can also be used to identify patterns. For example, a researcher can manually identify moves in the conclusion section of research articles and then use computer software to identify frequently occurring multi-word lexical expressions or grammatical structures in the data set. In this example, both strands of inquiry (manual and computer-software-based) have heuristic research objectives. They represent qualitative research as they seek to identify patterns or features. However, the researcher might add a further quantitative strand to the inquiry and try to determine whether the expressions or structures identified above are more frequent in a specific move.

Linguistic ethnography combines linguistic and ethnographic approaches as a means of understanding social and communicative processes in various contexts (Shaw, Copland & Snell, 2015). In EAP, ethnographic research endeavours to develop understanding of social influences on academic language use through inquiry to gain insights into insiders' experiences and views, and the contexts of use of academic texts (Paltridge, Starfield & Tardy, 2016). EAP has a long tradition of calling on such insiders to explain contexts and linguistic choices (Flowerdew, 2002). Such insiders are referred to as specialist informants, inside members or domain experts. Ethnographic inquiry of an academic context might include the collection of detailed observational data, transcriptions of speech events and semi-structured interviews with participants in the event (Bruce, 2011). In studies of academic writing, interviews can be held with student writers to discuss their writing samples. Or, a researcher conducting a genre analysis of the research article may discuss sample excerpts with the writers of articles, asking them to explain intentions and thinking behind their linguistic choices (Basturkmen, 2012).

Purely linguistic analysis seeks to generalise about language structure or use and is generally limited to examining what is said or written. Ethnography provides a mean of making a fundamentally linguistic project richer by reaching deeper into social or institutional processes (Rampton, Maybin & Roberts, 2015). For example, a study of a genre could combine inquiry into both context and text by either adopting a text-first or context-first approach (Paltridge, 2006). The researcher could start by examining a text sample of the genre in question to identify, for example, the typical move sequence (discourse structure) involved (text-first approach) or start with inquiry into the context in which the genre is used (context-first). An ethnographic study of the social and cultural context of academic genres could include examination of the setting of the text; the focus and perspective of the text; the purposes of the text; the intended audience for the text; the relationship between writers and readers of the text; expectations and conventions for the text; and the relationship of the text to other texts (Paltridge, Starfield & Tardy, 2016).

Three broad options for EAP linguistic inquiry are shown in Figure 2.5. As can be seen, the three options all concern text analysis and, in this sense, are all analyses of discourse. Even an investigation to establish the vocabulary a discipline has in EAP has typically been approached through analysis of words occurring in authentic texts from that discipline. (A researcher might ask subject experts to use introspection to identify words commonly used in their discipline, but this is unlikely to provide reliable data.) The third option is to include an ethnographic strand of inquiry to supplement the text analysis. The descriptions reported in the rest of this book are based largely on one or more of these options. A purely ethnographic approach to the study of academic texts is possible – for example, a researcher might investigate a genre only through interviews with members of the academic discourse community who produce and reproduce that genre in their work. However, in EAP in general, ethnography has been used along with discourse analysis.

2.5 Making Tacitly-held Knowledge Explicit

As described above, discourse analysis of naturally occurring academic texts produced by competent writers and speakers of academic English has been the methodological mainstay of EAP linguistic inquiry. It has been the basis for much of the description of academic English that is currently available. For example, numerous studies have used published research articles as their data.

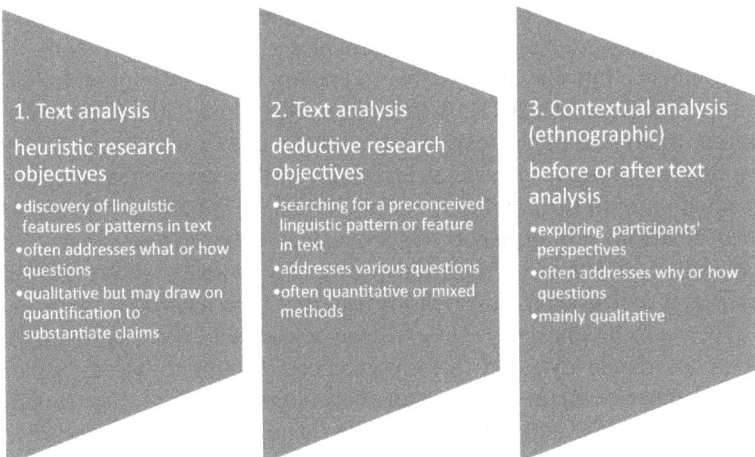

Figure 2.5 Forms of inquiry.

It is probable that relatively few of the writers of these research articles had much "explicit," declarative knowledge of the research article genre or had received explicit description or information about the uses of English in research-article writing. Explicit knowledge is factual knowledge, or the conscious understanding people have of language forms and features, which they can often express. It is likely that most of the writers had largely "tacit" knowledge acquired through exposure to academic English and routine encounters with research articles – tacit knowledge is "implicit" knowledge derived from implicit learning. On the other hand, teaching proposals, including those that appear in the end sections of many EAP reports of linguistic inquiry, tend to imply an explicit approach to teaching academic English in which learners will develop a conscious awareness of academic English – explicit knowledge derived from explicit learning (Basturkmen, 2020).

To test if a learner has acquired explicit knowledge, we might ask the learner to state whether a sentence is ungrammatical and explain why (Ellis, 2009). We could extend this to academic English and ask which of two versions of a text or text part – for example, a research article abstract or introduction to a student essay – is more academic in style or organisation and to explain why. EAP teaching reported in the literature generally refers to explicit instruction and suggests activities in which learners notice, analyse and describe genres or identify and discuss specific grammatical or lexical features of academic English.

Implicit knowledge is tacit or unconscious knowledge, which people are usually unaware of having and cannot necessarily explain. First-language speakers may be able to recognise a grammatical irregularity in a sentence but may not be able to explain why it is ungrammatical (Loewen & Reinders, 2011). Implicit learning occurs without the intention or awareness of the learner, who may be unaware of having learnt anything, although evidence of learning can be seen in their language production or in their ability to recognise correct appropriate language. In an academic setting, expert writers, such as seasoned researchers who have authored numerous research articles, may be able to judge whether a research article abstract is well-formed, and experienced lecturers and teachers may be able to recognise whether a student's essay has an appropriate, academic style. Yet these researchers, lecturers or teachers may not be able to explain the basis for their judgments. They have largely tacit knowledge of the genres, which they acquired through exposure to academic writing.

In summary, EAP linguistic research makes explicit the largely tacit knowledge of competent members of the academic discourse community in general, or specific, disciplinary discourse communities. This research describes academic English using evidence from texts produced by members, texts that are considered representative of the discourse practices across a wider population of writers and speakers in academic and research settings. Proposals for teaching academic English, on the other hand, often include activities to help learners develop an explicit knowledge of academic English.

References

Basturkmen, H. (2012). A genre-based investigation of discussion sections of research articles in dentistry and disciplinary variation. *Journal of English for Academic Purposes*, 11(2), 134–144.

Basturkmen, H. (2015). Introduction. In H. Basturkmen (Ed.), *English for academic purposes, vol. 3* (pp. 1–4). London: Routledge.

Basturkmen, H. (2020). Is ESP a materials and teaching-led movement? *Language Teaching*, 1–11. Doi: 10.1017/S0261444820000300.

Bloor, T. & Bloor, M. (1986). *Language for specific purposes: Practice and theory.* Occasional Paper 19. Dublin: Trinity College.

Bruce, I. (2011). *Theory and concepts of English for academic purposes.* Basingstoke: Palgrave Macmillan.

Cohen, L. & Manion, L. (1980). *Research methods in education* (3rd edition). London: Routledge.

Ellis, R. (2009). Implicit and explicit learning, knowledge and instruction. In R. Ellis, S. Loewen, C. Elder, E. Erlam, J. Philp & H. Reinders (Eds), *Implicit and explicit knowledge in second language learning, testing and teaching* (pp. 3–25). Bristol: Multilingual Matters.

Flowerdew, J. (2002). Ethnographically inspired approaches to the study of academic discourse. In J. Flowerdew (Ed.) *Academic discourse* (pp. 235–252). Abingdon, Oxon: Routledge.

Flowerdew, J. (2013). *Discourse in English language education*. London: Routledge.

Flowerdew, J. (2017). Corpus-based approaches to language description for specialised academic writing. *Language Teaching*, 50 (1): 90–106.

Herbert, A.J. (1965). *The structure of technical English*. London: Longman.

Hopper, P. (1987). *Emergent grammar*. Berkeley Linguistics Society, 13: 139–157.

Hyland, K. (2002). *Teaching and researching writing*. Harlow: Longman.

Hyland, K. (2006). *English for academic purposes: An advanced resource book*. London: Routledge.

Hymes, D. (1987). Communicative competence. In U. Ammon, N. Dittmar & K.J. Mattheier (Eds), *Sociolinguistics: An international handbook of the science of language and* society (pp. 219–229). Berlin: Walter de Gruyter.

Jaworski, A. & Coupland, N. (2014). *The discourse reader* (3rd edition). London: Routledge.

Johnstone, B. (2008). *Discourse analysis* (2nd edition). Oxford: Blackwell.

Loewen, S. & Reinders, H. (2011). *Key concepts in second language acquisition*. Basingstoke: Palgrave Macmillan.

Nesi, H. & Gardner, S. (2012). *Genres across the disciplines: Student writing in higher education*. Cambridge: Cambridge University Press.

Paltridge, B. 2006. Discourse *analysis*. London: Continuum.

Paltridge, B. & Wang, W. (2010). Researching discourse. In B. Paltridge & A. Phakiti (Eds), *Continuum companion to research methods in applied linguistics* (pp. 256–273). London: Continuum.

Paltridge, B., Starfield, S. & Tardy, C.M. (2016). *Ethnographic perspectives on academic writing*. Oxford: Oxford University Press.

Phakiti, A. & Paltridge, B. (2015). Approaches and methods in applied linguistics research. In B. Paltridge & A. Phakiti (Eds), *Research methods in applied linguistics* (pp. 1–26). London: Bloomsbury Academic.

Rampton, B., Maybin, J. & Roberts, C. (2015). Theory and method in linguistic ethnography. In J. Snell. S. Shaw & F. Copland (Eds) *Linguistic ethnography* (pp. 14–50). Basingstoke: Palgrave Macmillan.

Schiffrin, D, Tannen, D. & Hamilton, H.E. (2001). Introduction. In D. Schiffrin, D. Tannen & H.E. Hamilton (Eds), *The handbook of discourse analysis* (pp. 1–10). Oxford: Blackwell.

Seliger, H.W. & Shohamy, E. (1989). *Second language research methods*. Oxford: Oxford University Press.

Shaw, S., Copland, F. & Snell, J. (2015). An introduction to linguistic ethnography: Interdisciplinary explorations. In J. Snell, S. Shaw & F. Copland (Eds) *Linguistic ethnography: Interdisciplinary explorations* (pp. 1–13). Basingstoke: Palgrave Macmillan.

Swales, J.M. (1990). *Genre analysis: English in academic and research settings*. Cambridge: Cambridge University Press.
Swales, J.M. (2001). EAP-related linguistic research: An intellectual history. In J. Flowerdew & M. Peacock (Eds), *Research perspectives on English for academic purposes* (pp. 42–54). Cambridge: Cambridge University Press.
Swales, J.M. (2019). The future of EAP genre studies: A personal viewpoint. *Journal of English for Academic Purposes*, 38: 75–82.
Wells, G. (1992). The centrality of talk in education. In K. Norman (Ed.) *Thinking voices: The work of the national oracy project*. London: Hodder & Stoughton.

3 The General Academic English Register

3.1 Introduction

The impetus to provide language descriptions for teaching academic English has fuelled research to identify the grammar and vocabulary in the general academic English register. Research has sought to identify the linguistic constituents common to discourse across academic genres and disciplines. Descriptions of the general academic English register are of potential interest to a wide audience that includes content teachers and students in school and university settings, teachers of English for academic purposes and academics. The chapter describes ways this diverse audience might draw on findings from the research. It discusses the importance of inquiry into the grammatical and lexical constituents of academic style and describes the nature of the inquiry. The Studies in Focus section examines recent corpus-based studies that have investigated grammatical or lexical constituents of the general academic register. The studies include investigations into academic written style, an academic word list and an academic formulas list, and an inquiry into idioms in academic speaking and writing. Sample findings from the studies are given to illustrate the nature of the description they have provided.

Readers will recognise that, although sentences (a) and (b) on the next page convey a very similar message, sentence (b) is more characteristic of academic style than sentence (a). For most readers, recognition of this will be straightforward, as they can rely on their tacit knowledge of academic English (see discussion of tacit knowledge in Chapter 2). However, to be able to provide instruction on academic style or to comment on the academic style of others, teachers and researchers need "information about" the kinds of linguistic features that are and are not associated with it. An important thrust of linguistic inquiry in EAP has been to provide this kind of information, that is, to identify the kind of grammar and vocabulary that typify academic expression.

(a) When you don't eat right, you'll feel tired
(b) Continuous deprivation of essential nutrients is a major source of reduced energy levels

3.2 Importance of Description

If English for general academic purposes (EGAP) courses are to provide information about academic English in general they require descriptions of the general academic register. In teaching English for specific academic purposes (ESAP) the concern has been to impart information about disciplinary English (the disciplinary register), foster learners' development of that register including their abilities to read and write the types of texts used in study of that discipline. EGAP has generally been far more prevalent than ESAP, and globally there are many examples of EGAP courses in the initial years of tertiary education that aim to prepare students for future study. There are various reasons why EGAP has remained the dominant orientation in teaching. EGAP type courses are appropriate when students are new to higher education and may not yet have decided which discipline to study. From an institutional point of view, the provision of one or two general academic English courses suitable for students from varied disciplines can seem more practical and financially viable than provision of a raft of English courses for all the different disciplines. From the EAP teacher's viewpoint, EGAP can also be viewed as the most practical orientation since EAP teachers do not necessarily have a background in the various disciplines that the students may study.

Descriptions of academic English in general can be of value to teachers and lecturers in any discipline, not only English-language teachers. In many settings around the world, teachers and lectures are using English to teach their subjects. They may be interested in learning more about the linguistic means used to express ideas and information in an academic style. They respond to students' writing, and in doing so, may wish to comment on a student's grammatical and lexical choices, the accuracy of the grammar or the clarity (or lack of it). Knowledge about some of the linguistic features of academic style and terms used to talk about it, a metalanguage for linguistic items, can be useful in giving feedback. Teachers model academic language use, and their knowing about the constituents of the academic register may help them monitor, and possibly extend, their repertoires. Many help students with language during their content teaching. Recent research into classroom interaction in school and tertiary settings in English-speaking and in EMI contexts, shows that content teachers periodically "talk about" language during their classes. They take brief time outs from discussion of subject content to highlight language use, correct ways students linguistically formulate some utterances and respond to student queries about language (see discussion of EMI in Chapter 1).

For academics and those who write scholarly works, knowledge about the general academic register could help them in monitoring their academic writing. As argued in Chapter 2, they use this register in their writing. Seasoned academics and editors can often draw intuitively on a set of linguistic features to ensure that their academic writing meets these demands. They mostly have implicit knowledge of the typical linguistic constituents of academic writing style, or at least the ones that feature in their repertoire. Formality in academic writing is difficult to define (Liardét, Black & Bardetta, 2019). Descriptions of professional academic writing could help them in crafting and revising their writing, or in providing feedback comments on the writing of others. Descriptions of the typical grammatical constructions in the academic register could help them become more knowledgeable (develop explicit knowledge) about the linguistic constituents, which they can draw on in formulating alternative and possibly more sophisticated forms of expression.

3.3 The Nature of Description

Inquiry into the grammar and vocabulary of academic English continues a long tradition of research that began in the 1960s and 1970s – At that time this line of inquiry was referred to as lexical-grammatical research or lexico-grammatical statistics, the search for the grammatical features and vocabulary that characterised academic texts. Inquiry focused on texts from science and technology, as most EAP students at that time were from these disciplines. However, over the years, the focus shifted to academic English in general and thus inquiry into the grammatical features and vocabulary characteristic of English across a range of disciplines.

Theoretically, as argued in Chapter 2, it can be said that there is no general English register, but rather a multitude of academic registers depending on disciplines and genres. Inquiry to produce linguistic descriptions of the academic English register is generally based on identification of the formal features (grammar and vocabulary) in a data set that comprises texts from a range of disciplines and genres – a mixed data set of academic prose (writing) and in some cases academic speaking as well as prose. Some research has investigated the content of academic style manuals – see, for example, Bennet (2009). Although much present-day research is concerned with identification of linguistic features in specific academic disciplines and genres, it is understood that these draw on a largely similar repertoire of features commonly used in academic settings, and what distinguishes disciplines and genres is the frequency with which certain forms are used or the functions the forms carry in the specific disciplines or genres (Shaw, 2013).

Most recent linguistic inquiry into the general academic register has been based on corpus analysis. Corpus-based research has become increasingly prominent in EAP over the last two decades, and its findings have played a major role in the development of knowledge about how English is used for academic purposes. The nature of inquiry is essentially descriptive and uses corpus techniques to identify key features that distinguish academic language use from English language use in more general, everyday settings. Because of this, studies tend to identify linguistic features of the academic register by comparing a corpus compiled of texts from academic settings with a reference corpus compiled of texts from everyday settings. Yet other corpus-based research has compared academic writing and academic speaking (Biber, 2006; Liu & Myers, 2020).

Important insights have also been found in the broad descriptions of the academic register based on a synthesis of literature by key EAP scholars. Hyland (2009) compares academic writing to everyday language. In everyday language there is a tendency to make use of agents to accomplish actions and represent actions as events that unfold in a linear sequence. By contrast, academic writing often treats events as existing in cause-and-effect networks and foregrounds events, rather than people, as agents. These distinctions were reflected in (a) and (b) example sentences in the introduction of this chapter. Hewings, Lillis and Mayor (2007) describe further constituents of academic style – the disguising of authors' personal opinions or agency with third-person formulations (e.g. *it was of interest*) and the use of hedges to make claims cautiously (e.g. *it may be the case* rather than *it is the case*). Shaw (2013) identifies a range of features of academic writing that are specific to disciplines and genres. These include the use of the past tense to refer to results and procedures and the use of active voice for non-animate subjects (e.g. *the graph shows*) to thematise content.

3.4 Studies in Focus

This section reviews a selection of recent corpus-based inquiries into the formal features (grammatical and lexical forms) of the general academic English register. The first two studies largely concern style and grammatical aspects of academic writing, and the remaining three studies concern vocabulary (words, formulaic patterns and idioms).

3.4.1 Formal Style in Academic Writing

> Biber, D. & Gray. (2010). Challenging stereotypes about academic writing: Complexity, elaboration and explicitness. *Journal of English for Academic Purposes*, 9: 2–20.

What are some of the major differences in the grammar structures used in academic writing (academic prose) and everyday English? A perception that academic writing is structurally elaborate and explicit has long persisted. To investigate whether this perception reflects reality, Biber and Gray (2010) conducted a large-scale, corpus-based study to compare grammar structures in a corpus of academic writing – mostly research articles from a range of disciplines and university textbooks – and a corpus of everyday American English, – texts of naturally occurring, face-to-face conversations. The aim of the study was to establish if there was more use of elaborate grammar structures and more explicit expression of logical relations in the corpus of academic writing.

The study found that subordinate clauses, often seen as the hallmark of grammatical complexity, were more common in conversation than in academic writing, and there was no tendency toward explicit logical relations in academic writing. Rather, the study revealed that in academic writing there was a high frequency in the use of grammatical structures that required readers to infer relations between text elements. On the basis of their findings, the researchers concluded that academic writing should be described as a structurally compressed, rather than a grammatically complex, style and that "the 'compressed' discourse style of academic writing makes it much less explicit in meaning than alternative styles employing elaborated structures" (2).

As for specific findings, the study established that the most important structural feature of academic writing was the use of phrasal modifiers embedded in noun clauses. Sentences were elaborated through the (optional) use of a range of types of phrasal modifiers. The phrasal modifiers provided extra information in a much more compressed manner than lengthier clausal modifiers that provide fuller details (see Example 1).

> Example 1 from Biber & Gray (2010: 9):
> the *participant* perspective (phrasal modifier)
> the perspective *that considers the participant's point of view* (clausal modifier)

Table 3.1 Grammatical compression structures and implicit meanings

1 Grammatical structures frequent in academic writing	2 Examples	3 Comments
Passives & nominalisations	Passive: *Hazardous waste is managed* Nominalisation: *Hazardous waste management*	The agent is not explicit in the passive. That an event is occurring is not made explicit in the nominalisation.
Head noun & pre-modifying noun		The relationship between two nouns is not made explicit. The following clausal elaborations would make the relationship explicit.
	Heart disease	*A disease located in the heart*
	Alcohol consumption	*The process of consuming alcohol*
	Computation time	*The time needed to compute something*
Adjectives that pre-modify nouns	*Aspirin-resistant patients*	A noun (aspirin) is compounded with an adjective (resistant) and used to modify a head noun (patients), which sets up a series of implicit relations.

Source: Based on examples and discussion from Biber and Grey (2010: 11–12).

Table 3.1 shows pervasive features of grammatical compression in academic writing and explanations of why the structures convey implicit relations between text elements, leading to the need for readers to infer the nature of the relations. The structures associated with grammatical compression are listed in column 1. Example linguistic realisations are listed in column 2, and comments to explain how the "compressed" structures make the discourse much less explicit in meaning than alternative styles are given in column 3.

3.4.2 Features Associated with Informal Style

> Liardét, C.L., Black, S., Bardetta, V.S. (2019). Defining formality: Adapting to the abstract demands of academic discourse. *Journal of English for Academic Purposes*, 38: 146–158.

Student writers are often keenly aware of the expectation that their writing should have a formal academic style. Content teachers in schools and universities as well as EAP teachers often expend great effort in guiding their students towards a formal academic writing style. Yet, what are the constituents of formal academic style when it comes to student writing, and critically what linguistic constituents give the impression of or lack of an appropriate formal style? Liardét et al. (2019) compared the lexical and grammatical features in a set of disciplinary reports written by undergraduate students. In the first stage of the study, EAP instructors rated the reports on a scale of formality from 10 (high, proficient and consistent formal style) and 1 (low, inadequate informal style). In the second stage, reports that had been consistently rated high or low were used for a corpus-based analysis. The analysis searched the corpus to identify the occurrence of items from a list of linguistic features of formal and informal academic styles compiled with reference to the literature.

The analysis found a constellation of linguistic features that appeared to have given the impression of informality. These were categorised into four groups – grammatical errors, grammatical intricacy, informal vocabulary and "human interaction." Features associated with human interaction reflected the notion that formal academic expression presents "abstracted, non-human entities participating in impersonal activities ... and information organised as related events and processes" rather than personalised mental processes, the explicit involvement of human participants and direct interactions between them (150).

Findings revealed that the most significant attributes of highly rated samples was that the writing was error free, included appropriate use of vocabulary and the use of "lexically dense constructions" (nominalisations) and the absence of features of informal expression (extended clause coordination, prepositional phrases, de-lexical verbs, phrasal verbs and informal descriptors (156–157). Table 3.2 shows examples of these features of informal expression in the categories of human interaction and grammatical intricacy. The highly rated writing samples occasionally included some of the features associated with informal expression. By contrast, the low-rated samples included them on multiple occasions.

The sentence below illustrates some of the features shown in Table 3.2.

Officials now think the government must give up on this policy because it obviously results in less trade.

Table 3.2 Features associated with informal expression in human interaction and grammatical intricacy categories

Human interaction		Grammatical intricacy	
Human participants	e.g. *men, people*	Conjunctions	e.g. *so, but*
Opinion adverbs	e.g. *obviously, definitely*	Prepositions	e.g. *next to, after*
Obligation	e.g. *must, should*	Informal descriptors	e.g. *a lot, very many*
Personal mental processes	e.g. *believe, think*	De-lexical verbs	e.g. *get, have*
Verbal processes	e.g. *say, explain*	Phrasal verbs	e.g. *catch up, pass out*

Source: Liardét et al. (2019: 150).

Officials are human participants, *think* is a personal mental process, *must* is obligation, *give up on* is a phrasal verb, *because* is a conjunction and *obviously* is an opinion adverb.

3.4.3 Academic Word Families

> Coxhead, A. (2000). A new academic word list. *TESOL Quarterly*, 34(2): 213–238.

Research to identify core vocabulary that would be of value to English second language learners has a long history. The General Service List (GSL) (West, 1953) was one of the earliest attempts to identify useful words. The list, comprising two thousand English word families, was developed from a corpus of 5 million words, with criteria for selection including frequency, ease of learning and coverage. In the 1970s various academic word lists devised with the help of computers appeared, and four of these were combined and edited by Xue and Nation (1984) to create the University Word List (UWL), which at the time was widely adopted in EAP teaching and learning (Coxhead, 2000).

Coxhead (2000) devised the New Academic Word List (AWL) to provide a list of words that occur in many different types of academic texts and that could be used in various teaching and learning contexts, such as teachers setting vocabulary objectives in EAP courses and as a guide for materials developers in devising learning activities. Although, the concept of a general academic vocabulary has been contested (Hyland

& Tse, 2007), the AWL has remained an influential resource for teaching and learning academic English.

Coxhead's (2000) Academic Word List was based on the development and analysis of an academic corpus that comprised over four hundred texts divided into four sub-corpora of arts, commerce, law and science. It included a range of text types, such as articles, academic books, textbook chapters and university laboratory manuals. Coxhead identified word families in the corpus. Word families were defined as a word stem plus closely related affixed forms, for example, *legislate* (stem), *legislated, legislating, legislation, legislative, legislator, legislators, legislature* (related forms).

Selection of words for the AWL was based on three criteria:

- Specialised use: The words had to be outside the first 2,000 most frequently occurring words as identified by West (1953), that is, not words in general use
- Range: A member of a word family had to occur at least 10 times in each of the four sub corpora and in 15 subject areas
- Frequency: Members of the word family needed to occur at least 100 times in the academic corpus as a whole

The resulting AWL contains 570 word families, organised into frequency levels, with level 1 the highest and level 10 the lowest. These word families were found to account for around 10 per cent of the total words in the texts in the Academic Corpus, and only around 1.4 per cent of tokens in a comparable corpus of fiction texts. The AWL together with the first 2000 words in the GSL (West, 1953) was found to account for around 86 per cent of words in the Academic Corpus. Coxhead concluded that the AWL constitutes a specialised vocabulary with good coverage of academic texts, regardless of the subject area. Word families in level 1 of the AWL are shown in Table 3.3.

The AWL Coxhead (2000) has become a highly influential study. It illustrates a common core approach (Coxhead, 2013) in that it was an attempt to identify the words encountered in academic texts in general, rather than in a specific discipline.

3.4.4 Academic Formulas

> Simpson-Vlach, R. & Ellis, N.C. (2010). An academic formulas list: New methods in phraseology research. *Applied Linguistics*, 31(4): 487–512.

Table 3.3 Level 1 (most frequent) word families in the Academic Word List

Level 1 words (most frequent)
Analyse, Approach, Area, Access, Assume, Authority, Available, Benefit, Concept, Constant, Constitute, Context, Contract, Create, Data, Define, Derive, Distribute, Economy, Environment, Establish, Estimate, Evident, Export, Factor, Finance, Formula, Function, Identify, Income, Indicate, Individual, Interpret, Involve, Issue, Labour, Legal, Legislate, Major, Method, Occur, Per Cent, Period, Policy, Principle, Process, Require, Research, Respond, Role, Section, Sector, Significant, Similar, Source, Specific, Structure, Theory, Vary

Source: Coxhead (2000: 232–235).

Simpson-Vlach and Ellis (2010) aimed to establish an academic word list (for speech and writing) with the *Academic Formulas List* (487), based on a different approach than frequency alone. The aim was to provide a list of frequently occurring formulaic sequences (multi-word units) that drew on psychological and educational methods to ensure that the list would have clear pedagogical resonance. To this end, the researchers used additional methods to supplement their initial corpus analytical approach. Their spoken corpus was largely based on the Michigan Corpus of Academic Spoken English (MICASE), with the addition of selected files of the British National Corpus (BNC) of academic speech representing various speech events such as lectures and seminars. The written corpus included an existing corpus of research articles along with a selection of written academic genres from the BNC. Three-, four- and five-word strings (n-grams) were extracted from the data. The strings that were found to have occurred significantly more often in the academic corpus than in the corpus of everyday English, were subjected to two further analyses. The first was a measure of MI (mutual information), a statistical measurement used in information science to establish the extent to which the co-occurrence of items in the strings was more or less likely due to chance. The researchers argue that, although a string of words (an n-gram) may occur with a high frequency, this does not mean that it has a distinctive function or meaning that could be included in teaching academic English. For example, the string *this is the,* may occur frequently, but it is not functional or "pedagogically compelling" (493). By contrast, strings such as *trying to figure out* (academic speaking) and *due to the fact that* (academic writing), which were found to occur frequently in the corpus, and which had high MI scores, are recognisably meaningful and functional.

Hedges
mainly spoken: a kind of, it could be, it might be, might be able (to), a little bit about, it looks like, little bit about, you might want to, in a sense
mainly written: appear(s) to be, at least in, is likely to (be), it is likely that, are likely to, does not appear, it appears that, less likely to
written and spoken: (more) likely to (be), (it/there) may be, may not be, to some extent

Evaluation
mainly spoken: it doesn't matter
mainly written: important role in, it is important (to), it is necessary (to), (it) is clear (that), is consistent with, it is possible to, it is obvious that, the most important, it is difficult
written & spoken: the importance of

Source: Simpson-Vlach & Ellis (2010: 500–501).

Figure 3.1 The categories of hedges and evaluation in the AFL

To further ensure that strings the study identified through corpus analysis were educationally and psychologically valid, experienced EAP and ESL teachers were asked to judge whether the strings (the formulas) had functions that could be targeted in instruction. Those that did, were collated to make the *Academic Formulas List*. This list presents the formulas organised into functional categories and according to whether they were found in both academic writing and speaking, or in *either* academic writing or speaking. Two of the functional categories are illustrated in Figure 3.1. The figure shows formulas for hedging (a subcategory of stance) and for evaluation.

3.4.5 Academic Idioms

> Miller, J. (2020). The bottom line: Are idioms used in English academic writing and speech? *Journal of English for Academic Purposes*, 43.

It has been assumed that idioms are elements of informal style and do not appear in academic English. They would not, therefore, need to be taught in EAP instruction or highlighted by content teachers. Miller (2020) challenges this assumption with a study to investigate the incidence of idioms in academic English and whether idioms are used more in academic speaking than in academic writing. Idioms were defined as commonly recognised, syntactically "reasonably fixed," multiword expressions that carry figurative meaning that is "more or less" opaque

Table 3.4 Selection of idioms in academic speaking

Some frequent idioms in BASE	
On the other hand	In the long run
Bear in mind	Bad news
On the one hand	Driving force
The balance of power	On the face of it
At the end of the day	In (the) light of
On the other (hand)	Come into play
The bottom line	Gold standard
Take on board	What on earth
By and large	Go without saying
A step further/back	Trial and error
Take for granted	Down the line
In the hands of	Over the top
Along the lines of	State of the art
In its own right	The man/woman in the street
Across the board	Stepping-stone
At the back of one's mind	
Sit on the fence	

Source: Miller (2020: 9).

(2020: 4), for example, *bear in mind* and *on the one hand*. The study drew on two existing corpora – the British Academic Spoken English (BASE) corpus and the Oxford Corpus of Academic English (OCAE). Miller first identified idioms in BASE and then compared the frequency of the same set of idioms in OCAE. The analysis provided a list of over five hundred idioms, 56 of which appeared in four or more BASE (spoken texts) and 43 of which appeared more than a hundred times in OCAE (written texts). Findings from the study were used to provide lists of academic idioms. Miller argues that the listed idioms can be used with confidence by teachers, students and academic writers as they have been found to be frequent in academic texts. Table 3.4 shows a selection of frequently occurring idioms found in academic speaking.

References

Bennet, K. (2009). English academic style manuals: A survey. *Journal of English for Academic Purposes*, 8: 43–54.

Biber, D. (2006). *University language; A corpus-based study of spoken and written registers.* Amsterdam: John Benjamins.

Biber, D. & Gray. (2010). Challenging stereotypes about academic writing: Complexity, elaboration and explicitness. *Journal of English for Academic Purposes*, 9: 2–20.

Coxhead, A. (2000). A new academic word list. *Teaching English to Speakers of Other Languages Quarterly*, 34(2): 213–238.
Coxhead, A. (2013). Vocabulary and ESP. In B. Paltridge & S. Starfield (Eds), *The handbook of English for specific purposes* (pp. 115–132). Oxford: Wiley-Blackwell.
Hewings, A., Lillis, T. & Mayor, B. Academic writing in English. In N. Mercer, J. Swann & B. Mayor (Eds) (2007). *Learning English*. Abingdon, Oxon: Routledge.
Hyland, K. (2009). *Academic discourse; English in a global context.* London: Continuum.
Hyland, K. & Tse, P. (2007). Is there an "academic vocabulary"? *Teaching English to Speakers of Other Languages Quarterly*, 41(2): 235–253.
Liardét, C.L., Black, S., Bardetta, V.S. (2019). Defining formality: Adapting to the abstract demands of academic discourse. *Journal of English for Academic Purposes*, 38: 146–158.
Liu, D. & Myers, D. (2020). The most common phrasal verbs with their key meanings for spoken and academic written English: A corpus analysis. *Language Teaching Research*, 24(3): 403–424.
Miller, J. (2020). The bottom line: Are idioms used in English academic writing and speech? *Journal of English for Academic Purposes*, 43.
Shaw, P.M. (2013). Grammar in academic writing. In C.A. Chapelle (Ed.), *The encyclopedia of applied linguistics*. Oxford: Blackwell.
Simpson-Vlach, R. & Ellis, N.C. (2010). An academic formulas list: New methods in phraseology research. *Applied Linguistics*, 31(4): 487–512.
West, M. (1953). *A general service list of English words*. London: Longman.
Xue, G. & Nation, I.S.P. (1984). A university word list. *Language Learning and Communication*, 3: 215–229.

4 Study Genres and Events

4.1 Introduction

This chapter examines linguistic inquiry into the written genres that typically occur in the lives of students, such as assignments and spoken events, lectures and discussion classes. Participation in these genres and events are critical for student access to academic knowledge. Such genres and events serve as major means by which students develop their knowledge and understanding of their fields of study and are ultimately key for students' success in tertiary education.

Language serves as a major vehicle for teaching and learning. It is an important means of actualising teaching and learning. Yet, lecturers, teachers and students may have a vague understanding of the linguistic features and structures involved in study genres and events. Lecturers and teachers can often recognise that language use and organisation in students' assignments or presentations are not as required, but they may struggle to articulate the nature of the problem. They need a metalanguage about linguistic features that they can use to give feedback to students. They need to be able to make explicit their often implicit, or tacit, knowledge of linguistic features and organisations.

Some study genres and events, such as lectures and assignments, are common at undergraduate as well as postgraduate levels, whereas other genres, such as seminars, may be more common at the postgraduate level. Presentations and assignments are student productions, whereas lectures are largely produced by lecturers. Lectures, seminars, tutorials and laboratory classes are teaching genres. Certain events, such as seminars and office hours, are co-constructed by students and lecturers, as both play important roles in producing the discourse that emerges.

Student participation in some genres and events, especially written assignments, plays a major role in assessment. Assignments provide evidence of students' learning, as they are the means by which students demonstrate their understanding of topics in disciplinary

Table 4.1 Study genres and events

Written	Spoken
Student essays and other assignment genres	Lectures
Posts on web-based discussions	Discussions in seminars and tutorials
Textbooks	Office hour meetings
Applications for study	Student presentations
	Laboratory classes

Source: (Nesi & Gardner, 2012: 98).

study. Participation in seminars and office hours provides students with opportunities to ask questions and clarification checks to fine-tune their understanding of subject content and course requirements such as assignments, although students are not often assessed on their participation in such events per se. Table 4.1 shows some of the main written and spoken genres and events in the lives of students.

The focus of the present chapter is on the general structure and organisation of study genres and events. The Studies in Focus section includes three studies. These include two inquiries into events (lectures and discussion classes) and one set of study genres (student-assessed writing genres). The studies have provided description of the macrostructure or major features of the genres or events in question. Although the studies may have included some quantitative type of analysis, it is the qualitative thrust of inquiry that is reported in this chapter.

It is beyond the scope of the chapter to review the burgeoning body of literature on English second language students' development of the linguistic features or skills in study events and genres, students' perceptions of language in study genres and events, such as that of Lau, Cousineau and Lin (2016), or studies that investigated language use in genres and events in EAP instruction or writing tutorials, such as that of Wingate and Ogiermann (2019). It is recognised, however, that studies of second language learning and teaching are important topics for EAP.

4.2 Importance of Description

Linguistic description of study genres and events is of potential interest to those in the fields of Education, Applied Linguistics and EAP. However, the focus of interest may vary between these groups. Whereas researchers in Applied Linguistics may be interested in descriptions of study genres and events as social uses of language or as the focus of language acquisition studies, those in Education are more likely to draw on such descriptions when considering teaching and learning issues related to language use in educational settings. Disciplinary teachers and lecturers may draw on the metalinguistic terms in the descriptions to help them consider linguistic aspects of their teaching and in giving feedback to students.

Linguistic descriptions of key study genres and events can be drawn on by lecturers in higher education to better understand the forms of assessment they use and the kind of linguistic elements in them. Students may not be sure what their teachers expect. Appropriate organisation or expression may be included in assignment criteria. Yet, teachers and lecturers may not be able to articulate what this entails in concrete terms. Linguistic descriptions of an assignment genre, such as argumentative essays, can provide lecturers with explicit knowledge about the linguistic elements, and these can be communicated to students to help them better understand one of the criteria by which their writing will be assessed. Descriptions from genre analysis can provide metalinguistic terms that lecturers can use in providing details for assignments or grading criteria. For example, a lecturer might ask for an assignment that includes a literature review but not indicate what the review might include or how it might be structured. A genre-based description of literature reviews can provide the lecturer with terms that can be used to communicate expectations. Students are often required to demonstrate critical thinking in their work. Genre-based analysis by Bruce (2019) provides description that could help teachers and lecturers articulate their expectations for demonstration of critical thinking in student writing.

Similarly, lecturers might draw on categories and terms from genre analytic descriptions in giving feedback on the structure and organisation of assignments. Feedback comments on a student's essay, such as "Good introduction that sets out the *scope of the response*"; or "Introduction could be better if you include a *position statement at the end*," are more informative, as they indicate key content (scope and position statements) and organisation (at the end), than a comment that states simply "Introduction could have been better."

EAP teachers are likely to draw on the descriptions when devising pedagogical descriptions to use to help language learners navigate and participate in these complex genres and events, and in considering the kinds of difficulties such genres and events potentially pose for their learners. EAP teachers need, for example, to devise language descriptions for teaching and assessing students' academic speaking and writing (Newton et al., 2018), and to draw on the information from research when they produce study guides and materials. EAP teaching can include students from English first language backgrounds. In the initial year of university, all students, regardless of their first language,

Table 4.2 Questions for research and teaching

Education	*How is language used to highlight key points in lectures?* *What can I tell my students about organising essays and other kinds of assessed writing?* *How is information in textbooks typically organised?* *How do participants interact in tutorials and discussion classes?*
Applied linguistics	*How are study genres and events conventionally structured?* *How might conventional interaction patterns in teaching genres potentially disempower students?* *Does the practice of study genres and events vary across disciplines?* *How do learners acquire study genres?*
Teachers of English for academic purposes	*What can I tell my students about how study genres and events are organised?* *What can I tell my students about how language is used in study genres and events?* *What linguistic difficulties might my students have with study genres and events?* *What linguistic knowledge and skills do my students need to be ready for university study?*

are learning new academic genres and participating for the first time in study events. They may all benefit from the kind of information about study genres and events typically provided in EAP instruction. It has been argued (Feak, 2016: 493) that "all post-graduates, regardless of proficiency or L1, can benefit from EAP support," although not necessarily from semester-long courses. Both undergraduate and postgraduate students can benefit from workshops and one-to-one writing consultations that draw on descriptions of study genres.

Table 4.2 shows possible questions for researchers and teachers in Education, Applied Linguistics and EAP. The questions indicate reasons why researchers, lecturers and teachers might seek out and draw on linguistic descriptions of study genres and events. The list is not intended to be comprehensive, and the questions suggested for one discipline could be of interest to researchers and teachers in another.

4.3 Nature of Description

A selection of EAP literature on study genres and events is given in Table 4.3. The selection includes recent empirical studies and syntheses

Table 4.3 Selection of recent literature on study genres and events

Topic	Authors	Focus
Student essays and assessed writing	Graves & White (2016)	Assignments and essay exams – synthesis of literature
	Nesi & Gardner (2012)	Genres of assessed student writing
	Parkinson (2019)	Learner diaries
	Wingate (2012)	Argument structure
Lectures	Camiciottoli & Querol-Julian (2016)	Interactive linguistic features – synthesis of literature
	Camiciottoli (2007a)	Questions in lectures
	Deroey (2015)	Importance markers
	Deroey & Taverniers (2011)	Language functions
	Deroey & Taverniers (2012)	Relevance markers
	Wingrove (2017)	Vocabulary, lexical density and speech rate
	Camiciottoli (2007b)	Language of lectures
	Camiciottoli (2020)	Linguistic features in OpenCourseWare type lectures
Teacher talk	Csomay (2007)	Linguistic features in teacher vs. student talk
	Cotos & Chung (2019)	Language functions in teaching assistant talk
Discussion in seminars & tutorials	Basturkmen (2003)	Interaction
	Coxhead & Dang (2019)	Vocabulary in tutorials and laboratory classes
	Aguilar (2004)	Genre structure
	Aguilar (2016)	Interactive features and genre structure – synthesis of literature
	Basturkmen (2016)	Dialogic interaction – synthesis of literature
	O'Boyle (2014)	*You* and *I* for marking stance
Office hour and advisory meetings	Björkman, B. (2016)	PhD advisor-student interaction – synthesis of literature
Student presentations	Zareva (2016)	Vocabulary
Student applications for study	Chiu (2016)	Genre structure of personal statements
	Cadman (2002)	Genre structure of research proposals
Textbooks	Bondi (2016)	Genre structure – synthesis of literature

of literature. This section discusses research methodologies with reference to the empirical studies shown in the table.

In recent years, research into study writing has mainly drawn on a genre-based approach (Nesi & Gardner, 2012; Chiu, 2016; Parkinson, 2019). Genre-based approaches can be used to classify text types. A key focus of Nesi and Gardner's study was to identify and classify the genres of assessed student writing in UK universities. Parkinson (2019) reports a study of diaries, a key learning genre in the vocational education setting that she investigated, and a hitherto a largely little-known type of student writing. Chiu (2016) and Parkinson (2019) drew on the approach to genre analysis developed by Swales (1990). A major focus of such research is to identify the schematic structure of the genre or genres in question, that is, to identify the sequence of moves by which the genre is typically constructed. A move is a specific stretch of language that serves a specific communicative function. Genre-based approaches involve examining multiple examples of a targeted genre with the aim of identifying the conventional pattern or sequencing of moves involved and labelling the moves in terms that convey their content type or purpose in the text. For example, Chiu's (2016) study of personal statements in doctoral applications in Education was based on examination of over twenty applications for doctoral study in the United States and UK. The study identified a five-move schematic structure. Nesi and Gardner (2012), one of the studies reviewed in section 4.4 below, identified "stages" in genres of student-assessed writing in line with the genre approach of the Sydney School of Systemic Functional Linguistics and the definition of genres as "staged goal-oriented social processes through which social subjects in a given culture live their lives" (Martin, 1997: 13).

Whether one or another approach to genre analysis is adopted, studies in this area have provided descriptions of the sequential organisation, or schematic structure, of a genre based on evidence from multiple authentic samples of the genres. The resulting description shows the conventional pattern of organisation and the type of content typically included in the various moves or stages. Moves (or stages) can further be classified as obligatory (nearly always present) or optional (often present), based on evidence that the move occurred regularly in the samples examined. It is common for cut-off rates to be given for moves labelled obligatory (e.g. over 80 per cent of samples) and optional (e.g. over 50 per cent of samples).

Some research has focused on a speech act, or function. Pun (2019) investigated types of explanations in high school chemistry textbooks. Explanations had been found to be the most pervasive function in the textbooks. Five subcategories of explanations (causal, factorial, sequential, consequential and theoretical) and their salient linguistic features were identified by the researcher.

The kind of corpus-based research described in Chapter 3 has also been used in investigations of study genres and events, with research aiming to establish the frequency of linguistic forms in a corpus or corpora of texts of the genre or event in question. The frequency of multi-word units in university textbooks (Wood & Appel, 2014) and student academic presentations (Zareva, 2016) has been investigated. Corpus-based research has been used in inquiries into lecture discourse (Camiciottoli, 2020; Deroey, 2015; Deroey & Taverniers, 2012), student assessed writing (Nesi & Gardner, 2012) and seminars and tutorials (O'Boyle, 2014). For example, O'Boyle (2014) investigated the incidence and uses of *you* and *I* for indicating stance in a corpus of university seminar talk. Some researchers have conducted comparative inquiries. Coxhead and Dang (2019) compared vocabulary in tutorials compared to laboratory classes, and Csomay (2007) compared a range of linguistic elements in teacher talk compared to student talk.

A genre-based approach can be used to investigate spoken events (Aguilar, 2004). However, not all researchers have used this approach. A genre-based approach is arguably most suited to discourse that progresses in a largely linear way, which is often not the case in dialogue and multi-party speaking. Other approaches have been used to investigate academic speaking, including, analysis of speech acts, or functions (Cotos & Chung, 2019, Deroey & Taverniers, 2011) and interaction patterns (Basturkmen, 2000; 2003).

4.4 Studies in Focus

The works reviewed in this section have aimed to provide linguistic description of student written genres, seminar interaction and speech functions in lectures. The section includes focuses on interaction patterns and overall structure or major functions. The aim here is to report the findings relating to macro elements, elements underlying discourse, rather than findings relating to linguistic features on the surface of the discourse.

4.4.1 Student Genres of Assessed Writing

Nesi, H. & Gardner, S. (2012). *Genres across the disciplines: Student writing in higher education.* Cambridge: Cambridge University Press.

This book reports a study that involved the collation of a large corpus of assessed student writing across more than thirty disciplines and four years of study (year one, undergraduate, to year four, taught postgraduate). The corpus comprised samples of student assignments in their disciplines that had received good grades (a merit or distinction grade), which were collected at four UK universities. With reference to the samples, the researchers identified 13 families of genre writing and, drawing on a genre-based approach, they provide a descriptive account of the rhetorical organisation of the genres. Using corpus-analytic methods, they provide details about language use, such as keywords and grammatical features in the genres, to show ways genre practices vary across disciplines. In addition to the textual data, the study drew on contextual information – including interviews with university teaching staff and students and descriptions of the modules or courses of the targeted disciplines – in order to provide descriptions of the social purposes of the genres, or their educational function.

Genre families were distinctive in terms of their social (educational) purposes and their rhetorical organisation (sequential stages). Thirteen genre families were identified – *case study, critique, design specification, empathy writing, essay, exercise, explanation, literature survey, methodology recount, narrative recount, problem question, proposal and research report* (see Table 4.4). As shown in the table, the main purpose of genres in the *explanation* and *exercise* genre families is for students to develop and demonstrate their understanding. These genres are often used in the initial years of disciplinary study.

A wealth of detailed information about each of the genre families is provided by this research. I will illustrate the kind of description provided in this work with reference to a selection of the qualitative information it provides on the *essay* genre family. Essays generally have the aim of "developing an argument" but members of this differ in the way the argument evolves (Nesi & Gardner, 2012: 98). Table 4.5

Table 4.4 Social functions of genres of assessed student writing

Social function	To develop & demonstrate knowledge & understanding	To develop & demonstrate independent reasoning	To develop & demonstrate skills of research	To prepare for professional practice	Writing for self & for others
Genre families	Explanation Exercise	Critique Essay	Literature survey Methodology recount Research report	Case study Design specification Problem question Proposal	Narrative recount Empathy writing

Source: Based on Nesi & Gardner (2012: 36).

Table 4.5 Six Essay genres with stages.

Genres	exposition	discussion	challenge	factorial	consequential	commentary
genre stages	thesis,	issue,	challenge,	state,	state, ensuing	text(s)
	evidence,	alternative	evidence,	contri-	factors,	introduction,
	restate	arguments,	thesis	butory	summary	comments,
	thesis	final position		factors,	thesis	summary
				summary		
				thesis		

Source: (Nesi & Gardner, 2012: 98).

shows the six members of the essay family identified in the study and the stages of rhetorical organisation that each member was observed to include.

Essays and *critiques*, are distinct from *explanations* in that it is expected that each essay will be individual as the student writers develop different arguments. Essay genres were found to differ across disciplines. For example, there was a wider range of essay genres in History than in Sociology and Engineering. In History, students wrote *exposition, discussion, challenge* and *factorial* type essays, whereas in Sociology and Engineering they wrote *exposition* and *discussion* type essays. The book illustrates essay questions and rubrics from a range of disciplines and expectations for essay writing practice in them.

Amongst a rich array of linguistic description of *essays*, the work includes information on how student writers introduce themes, what they typically include in the first and final sentences of paragraphs in the main body, the function of frequent lexical bundles (such as *this shows that*), first-person forms and keywords. For example, *assert, portray* and *criticise* are amongst the key verbs identified in undergraduate essays. Description is provided about the organisation and content of essay introductions. The argument to be developed in the body of the assignment often begins "in the first few words of the first sentence, where a particular focus or slant on a topic is introduced" (Nesi & Gardner, 2012: 107), which is illustrated in the opening sentences below.

> Examples from Nesi and Gardner (2012: 107–108)
> **The Dutch Republic** was something of an anomaly in seventeenth century Europe.
> **Examination of the subcellular distribution of molecules** is an important tool in cell biology.

There are several different theories about what truth actually is, however, *truth in this essay is being taken as* agreement with reality (Philosophy Essay).

4.4.2 Functions in Lecturer Talk

Deroey, K.L.B. & Taverniers, M. (2011). *A corpus-based study of lecture functions*. Moderna Språk, 105(2): 1–22.

Lectures are without doubt one of the central instructional genres in higher education. They serve not only as a means for transmitting knowledge, but they also facilitate learning by arousing interest and stimulating thought, and they socialise novice students into the ways of thinking and attitudes of their disciplinary, professional or vocational communities. Surprisingly, linguistic description of lectures has been limited, and most research has focused on a limited selection of lexical and grammatical features on the surface of the discourse (Deroey & Taverniers, 2011). This research aimed to provide a comprehensive classification of the functions of lecturer language use, that is the underlying functions that motivate language use in lectures. The study was a qualitative analysis of a set of lectures from the British Academic Spoken English (BASE) corpus. To provide a cross-section of academic practice, lectures were drawn from four broad disciplinary fields, from level 1 undergraduate to postgraduate and from small to large lectures that ranged between seven to over a hundred participants.

In the initial stage of analysis, one sample lecture transcript from each disciplinary group was analysed for discourse functions in lecturer's talk. This involved a close reading of the transcript and efforts to identify the function of stretches of discourse. The researchers explain that although the analysis was guided by lexical and grammatical clues, a "degree of subjective interpretation is inevitable in the pragmatic coding of discourse" (4). The analysis was based on observations made of the lecture transcripts alone. It did not involve analysis of non-verbal communication. Figure 4.1 shows lecture functions and subfunctions identified in the study.

To illustrate, Excerpt 1 shows a stretch of discourse from a Chemistry lecture. It was coded as serving an overall *exemplification* function. Within this stretch, smaller linguistic units (embedded functions) were evident. One smaller unit is "so for example you could take lithium metal" which serves an *organise the discourse* function by signalling the exemplification and another is *what should we say* which is a hesitation device that serves a *manage the delivery* of the lecture function:

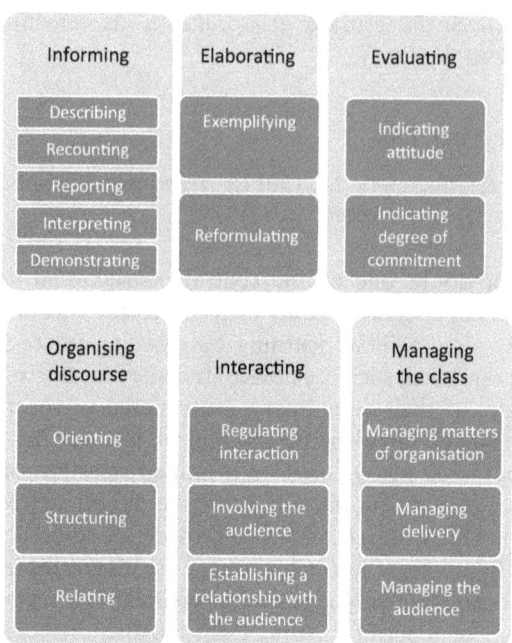

Figure 4.1 Lecture functions and subfunctions.
Source: Based on Deroey & Taverniers (2011: 5).

Excerpt 1: From Deroey & Taverniers (2011: 4)

So for example you could take lithium metal plus *what should we say* you could take ethyl bromide and what you would get out of that assuming that you used the condition above you had a dry atmosphere dry solvents and all the rest of it you would get lithium bromide.

In places, a stretch of discourse appeared to serve more than one function. This is illustrated in Excerpt 2. Here the discourse serves both a *managing the audience* and, as an attempt to create rapport, an *establish a relationship with the audience* function.

Excerpt 2: From Deroey and Taverniers (2011: 4)
I'm not feeling too good so I hope I survive this lecture.

The work describes the functions and subfunctions. To illustrate, *elaborating* occurs as lecturers make efforts to help students understand information, and its use reflects lecturers' assessment of their students' needs. The researchers distinguish two subcategories of elaborating – *exemplifying* and *reformulating*. These subfunctions were often, but not always, signalled linguistically with cues, such as *for instance*, in exemplifications and *what I mean* in reformulations, and *as you know* to draw on students' experiences in exemplifications. Lexical and grammatical markers of lecture functions are described in further works by the researchers (Deroey, 2015; Deroey & Taverniers, 2012).

4.4.3 Discussion Class Interaction

>Basturkmen, H. (2003). So what happens when the tutor walks in? Some observations on interaction in a university discussion group with and without the tutor. *Journal of English for Academic Purposes,* 2: 21–33.

Discussion-based classes play an important role in higher education, especially in higher levels of undergraduate study and in postgraduate study. Names for discussion-based classes vary, and terms such as *seminar*, *tutorial* and *discussion* classes are often used interchangeably across settings. Seminars in some settings are more formal events and can include student or guest-speaker presentation. However, the expectation is usually that there will be dialogic or multi-party interaction when participants ask and answer questions and give different points of view. Even when there is a presentation stage, the presentation is expected to serve as a springboard for discussion.

Dialogue is seen in education as a means of promoting learning through talking. Dialogic speaking is distinct from lectures, which often largely include monologue and the transmission of information and ideas. Through dialogue and multi-party discussion, ideas can be collaboratively developed, and ideas emerge through the process of discussion. Discussion is understood to play a role in deep processing of ideas and information. As we discuss ideas, we may come to refine our thinking on a topic. The process of discussion can act as a trigger for developing our ability to articulate ideas (Basturkmen, 2016). Despite the prevalence of discussion-based classes (and discussion interludes within lectures) research to build linguistic description of these events has been limited. One reason for this is the difficulty of analysing dialogue or multi-party interaction, which often appears unpredictable and lacking in any discernible organisation. Even question-and-answer routines are not necessarily simple two-part structures that can easily be analysed and classified.

Basic exchange structure (Coulthard & Brazil, 1992)

Speaker 1: I Initiation move
Speaker 2: R Response move
Speaker 1: (F) Optional follow up move

Extended exchange structure in discussion classes

Speaker 1: I Initiation
Speaker 2: R Response
Speaker 1: F/I Follow up as initiation
Speaker 2: R Response
Speaker 1: (F) Follow up

F/I move registers the preceding response as insufficient.
The F/I - R sequence can re-occur.

Figure 4.2 Interaction patterns in tutorial discussion.
Source: Based on Basturkmen (2000; 2003).

Basturkmen (2003) examined a discussion group before and after the unexpected arrival of the tutor. At first, several students were discussing the tutorial set questions in a peer-group discussion, in which no one student appeared to lead or control. Halfway through, the tutor unexpectedly arrived and began to lead the discussion. The analysis drew on *exchange structure* (Coulthard & Brazil, 1992), an approach to analysis of interaction in institutional settings, such as education. In this approach, an exchange is the basic unit of interaction in two- or multi-party talk. An *exchange* comprises, minimally, an *initiating move* by Speaker 1 and a *responding move* by Speaker 2 (see Figure 4.2). Following the response, there is an optional follow-up.

The study found that the interaction of the student peer-group discussion could not be analysed for initiation–response sequences, as the elements of exchange structure did not apply. To illustrate, Student 1 appears to answer his own question (responds to his own initiation) in Excerpt 3. The discussion before the tutor arrived was not in the form of statement–counter statement or question-and-answer type interaction.

Rather, the students added their ideas, but few of these were responded to or commented on by the others and were possibly not intended to elicit a response.

> Excerpt 3 from Basturkmen (2003: 26)
>
> Student 1: So, what do you think the source of innovation is? I think it is more the need that exists in the company.
>
> Student 2: Yeah, I thought that the need, the latent need, was there in the airline companies for an information system.

Once the tutor arrived, exchange structures became evident. The tutor initiated approximately half of the exchanges. In these exchanges, the follow-up move appeared to play an important role in teaching. The tutor used a follow-up move either to launch into providing information on the topic, or to register dissatisfaction with a student's response and guide the student towards the response that the tutor had in mind. In the latter, the follow-up move served to reinitiate, and thus extend the exchange, and was termed F/I, follow up as initiation (see Figure 4.2). The use of follow up to reinitiate and thus extend an exchange is illustrated in Excerpt 4.

> Excerpt 4 (Basturkmen, 2003: 29)
> Student (R): They were users, they were current users, one was a pilot and one was a musician, and they both developed, they both understood a need, a personal need, and they developed that as a commercial.
> Tutor: (F/I) So you found a variable in terms of user-dominated innovation?
> Student: (R): Yeah.
> Tutor (F/I): So, there's two instances of that?
> Student: (R) Yeah
> Tutor: F/I Okay, so, can you see the slight distinction between the two thoughts within that?
> Student: (R) Um, I think so.

References

Aguilar, M. (2004). The peer seminar, a spoken research process genre. *Journal of English for Academic Purposes*, 2: 55–72.
Aguilar, M. (2016). Seminars. In K. Hyland & P. Shaw (Eds), *The Routledge handbook of English for academic purposes* (pp. 335–347). London: Routledge.

Basturkmen, H. (2000). The organisation of discussion in university settings. *Text*, 20: 249–269.

Basturkmen, H. (2003). So what happens when the tutor walks in? Some observations on interaction in a university discussion group with and without the tutor. *Journal of English for Academic Purposes*, 2: 21–33.

Basturkmen, H. (2016). Dialogic interaction. In K. Hyland & P. Shaw (Eds), *The Routledge handbook of English for academic purposes* (pp. 152–164). London: Routledge.

Bondi, M. (2016). Textbooks. In K. Hyland & P. Shaw (Eds), *The Routledge handbook of English for academic purposes* (pp. 323–334). London: Routledge.

Björkman, B. (2016). PhD advisor and student interaction as a spoken academic genre. In K. Hyland & P. Shaw (Eds), *The Routledge handbook of English for academic purposes* (pp. 348–360). London: Routledge.

Bruce, I. (2019). Exploring critical thinking in academic and profession writing: A genre-based approach. In K. Hyland & L.L.C. Wong (Eds), *Specialised English: New directions in ESP and EAP research and practice* (pp. 107–119). London: Routledge.

Cadman, K. (2002). English for academic possibilities: The research proposal as a contested site in postgraduate pedagogy. *Journal of English for Academic Purposes*, 1: 85–104.

Camiciottoli, B.C. (2007a). Interaction in academic lectures vs. written text materials: The case of questions. *Journal of Pragmatics*, 40: 1216–1231.

Camiciottoli, B.C. (2007b). *The language of business studies lectures*. Amsterdam: John Benjamins.

Camiciottoli, B.C. (2020). The OpenCourseWare lecture: A new twist on an old genre? *Journal of English for Academic Purposes*, 46.

Camiciottoli, B.C. & Querol-Julián, M. (2016). Lectures. In K. Hyland & P. Shaw (Eds), *The Routledge handbook of English for academic purposes* (pp. 309–322). London: Routledge.

Chiu, Y-L., T. (2016). "Singing your tune" Genre structure and writer identity in personal statements for doctoral applications. *Journal of English for Academic Purposes*, 21: 48–59.

Cotos, E. & Chung, Y-R. (2019). Functional language in curriculum genres: Implications for testing international teaching assistants. *Journal of English for Academic Purposes*, 41: 100766.

Csomay, E. (2007). A corpus-based look at linguistic variation in classroom interaction: Teacher talk versus student talk in American university classes. *Journal of English for Academic Purposes*, 6: 336–355.

Coulthard, M. & Brazil, D. (1992). Exchange structure. In M. Couthard (Ed.), *Advances in spoken discourse analysis* (pp. 50–78). London: Routledge.

Coxhead, A. & Dang, T.N.Y. (2019). Vocabulary in university tutorials and laboratories. In K. Hyland & L.L.C. Wong (Eds), *Specialised English: New directions in ESP and EAP research and practice* (pp. 120–134). London: Routledge.

Deroey, K.L.B. (2015). Marking importance in lectures: Interactive and textual orientations. *Applied Linguistics*, 36(1): 51–72.

Deroey, K.L.B. & Taverniers, M. (2011). A corpus-based study of lecture functions. *Moderna Språk*, 105(2): 1–22.

Deroey, K.L.B. & Taverniers, M. (2012). Just remember this: Lexicogrammatical markers in lectures. *English for Specific Purposes*, 31: 221–233.

Feak, C.B. (2016). EAP support for post-graduate students. In K. Hyland & P. Shaw (Eds), *The Routledge handbook of English for academic purposes* (pp. 489–501). London: Routledge.

Graves, R. & White, S. (2016). Undergraduate assignments and essay exams. In K. Hyland & P. Shaw (Eds), *The Routledge handbook of English for academic purposes* (pp. 297–308). London: Routledge.

Lau, K., Cousineau, J. & Lin, C-Y. (2016). The use of modifiers in English-medium lectures by native speakers of Mandarin: A study of student perceptions. *Journal of English for Academic Purposes*, 21: 110–120.

Martin, J.R. (1997). Analysing genre: Functional parameters. In F. Christie & J.R. Martin (Eds), *Genres and institutions: Social processes in the workplace and school* (pp. 3–39). London: Continuum.

Nesi, H. & Gardner, S. (2012). *Genres across the disciplines: Student writing in higher education*. Cambridge: Cambridge University Press.

Newton, J., Ferris, D., Goh, C, Grabe, W., Stoller, F.L., & Vandergrift, L. (2018) (Eds) *Teaching English to second language learners in academic contexts*. Abingdon, Oxon: Routledge.

O'Boyle, A. (2014). "You" and "I" in university seminars and spoken learner discourse. *Journal of English for Academic Purposes*, 16: 40–56.

Parkinson, J. (2019). Multimodal student texts: Implications for ESP. In K. Hyland & L.L.C. Wong (Eds) *Specialised English: New directions in ESP and EAP research and practice* (pp. 149–161). London: Routledge.

Pun, J.K.H. (2019). Salient language features in explanation texts that students encounter in secondary school chemistry textbooks. *Journal of English for Academic Purposes*, 42:

Swales, J.M. (1990). *Genre analysis: English in academic and research settings*. Cambridge: Cambridge University Press.

Wingate, U. (2012). "Argument!" helping students understand what essay writing is about. *Journal of English for Academic Purposes*, 11: 145–154.

Wingate, U. & Ogiermann, E. (2019). Directives in academic writing tutorials. In K. Hyland & L.L.C. Wong (Eds), *Specialised English: New directions in ESP and EAP research and practice* (pp. 228–239). London: Routledge.

Wingrove, P. (2017). How suitable are TED talks for academic listening? *Journal of English for Academic Purposes*, 30: 79–95.

Wood, D.C. & Appel, R. (2014). Multiword constructions in first year business and engineering university textbooks and EAP textbooks. *Journal of English for Academic Purposes*, 15: 1–13.

Zareva, A. (2016). Multi-word verbs in student academic presentations. *Journal of English for Academic Purposes*, 23: 83–98.

5 Professional Research Genres and Events

5.1 Introduction

The genres and events examined in this chapter play important roles in research and publication processes. They are genres written by researchers for researchers, and events where researchers speak to other researchers. Research-grant applications, for example, may play a key role at the outset of the research cycle, and their outcome determines whether an idea for research becomes an actual research project. In some disciplines, research requires such high levels of expenditure and time that a sole researcher is highly unlikely to undertake research without the kind of financial support and staffing allocations that research grants can provide. This is usually the case in science fields and often the case in Social Sciences and Education as well. In other disciplines, such as Humanities, some research projects may be conducted by the sole researcher, whose main concern can be time to complete the project. Conference presentations also play a key role in the research process. Researchers may use this genre to showcase their work or, if the research is on-going, to gain audience feedback, fresh perspectives on their topic or indications of which aspects of the research seem to engender the most interest from the audience. Publication of research is increasingly seen as the hallmark of success in research, and most academics feel keenly the demands to publish that research. As a result, research articles (RAs), book chapters and book-length monographs are generally accomplishments that academics value highly. These publication genres play an important role in the later stages or after the research cycle.

This chapter focuses on EAP linguistic inquiry and description of professional research genres. It does not include inquiries into student research genres, such as theses and dissertations, unless these were studies that compared student research genres to professional research genres.

Professional Research Genres and Events 63

There is a growing body of research evidence to indicate that theses and dissertations are distinctive from research articles (Basturkmen, 2009; El-Dakhs, 2018; Koutsantoni, 2006; Kwase, 2015) in terms of the different roles of the writer and the power relationship between the writer and reader as well as the different functions of the thesis or dissertation compared to the RA. They can be considered as educational or pedagogical, rather than research genres. The Studies in Focus section includes an inquiry into conference proposals, one into RA introduction, and one of discussions at the end of conference presentations. All three inquiries involved a comparative thrust of investigation to identify possible differences between groups of writers or between the genre or event in question and a second, related genre or event.

5.2 Importance

English has become firmly established as the international academic lingua franca. English has become the choice language of academic publishing – the *lingua franca of academic publishing*. Having one common academic language allows English-speaking readers access to a globally produced body of disciplinary literature. There can be a greater sharing of research knowledge as the role of English as the global academic lingua franca becomes entrenched. Having one shared language also smooths the way for international research collaboration and publication.

The ability to function and thrive in a professional academic position is one that typically involves participation in a complex system of communicative academic, research-oriented practices (Belcher, Serrano & Yang, 2016). EAP literature on the topic of language use in such practices has increased dramatically in recent years, so much so that the terms *English for Professional Academic Purposes* (EPAP) or *English for Research Publication Purposes* (ERPP) have emerged in recognition of the topic's status as a sub specialism of EAP. Although the need for those with academic positions as lecturers, professors and research fellows to "publish or perish" is not new, the requirement to publish has never been as trenchantly applied as in recent times. Universities across the world require staff to present their research at international conferences and, more significantly, to publish their research in major, high-impact Anglophone journals as a precondition for tenure and promotion (Hyland, 2009). Academic job applicants, too, are often at pains to demonstrate their publication achievements, and academic jobs are often advertised in such a way as to preclude applicants without a demonstrable track record in research publication from applying. Academic publishing, once seen as the means of participating in scholarly conversations and contributing to disciplinary knowledge, has come to be perceived by many academics as "a necessary exercise in personal professional branding" (Belcher et al., 2016: 503).

There are social reasons why the pressure to publish is so paramount. Publication in influential international journals allows researchers to gain recognition through achieving international visibility in their disciplines. Their research is showcased for a global disciplinary audience. For potential readers, the rigorous peer review and selection processes of top-tier journals provide clear indicators of the merit of the research and quality of the study. For marketing purposes, universities have become increasingly concerned with publicising their global rankings, and one major element in these rankings is the number of faculty publications in leading international journals (Belcher et al., 2016). Flowerdew (2019) highlights the neoliberal view of the university, which has largely come to replace the traditional view of the university as a site for scholarly exploration. In the neoliberal view, the university is a market-driven entity that competes with other universities to attract students and government funding. This entity tends to adopt a style of governance that emphasises efficiency, accountability and control. In line with this focus on accountability and control, the university implements a system of surveillance and measurement of research productivity, often calculated by numbers of research publications by faculty in high-impact international journals. Many universities around the world have adopted English as their medium of instruction in the drive to compete for increasingly mobile students in the global marketplace.

It has been estimated that plurilingual users of English as an additional language now outnumber first-language English speakers three to one (Pérez-Llantada, 2012; Belcher et al., 2016). However, this does not appear to have resulted in an increase in tolerance for representations of academic knowledge in ways that do not align with Anglocentric norms and little acceptance of diversity in the practices of academic publishing. EAP scholars have expressed concerns that publishing in the prestigious international journals can present an unfair disadvantage for researchers using English as their second, or a foreign, language (Swales, 2004; Flowerdew, 2013). These users of English as an additional language (EAL) not only have to function in a second language but are often far removed from the networking opportunities of the inner-circle (Kachru, 1982) researchers. EAL researchers in less economically developed regions, too, may lack the kind of material and intellectual support enjoyed by many researchers in inner-circle settings

(Belcher et al., 2016) that can help them navigate the rocky terrain of academic publishing. One of the major benefits of linguistic inquiry into professional research genres is that findings can be used to help EAL researchers trying to publish research reports or to present conference papers in English. EAP teachers armed with linguistic descriptions of publication and presentation genres "would seem well-positioned to step into the breach and address some EAL researchers' needs" (Belcher et al., 2016: 503). Some universities provide research publication support, such as English-language consultants, translation and editing services and access to writing centres or retreats. Findings from linguistic inquiry into professional research genres can be of relevance to such consultants and those working in research writing centres. Linguistic description of research genres is of potential interest to English first-language researchers also. Novice research writers, regardless of first language background, may struggle to understand the rhetorical expectations for a specific section of a research article or conventional ways of framing a research grant application. It is these kinds of needs that have prompted much of the EAP linguistic inquiry into professional research genres.

5.3 Nature of Inquiry

5.3.1 Orientations

Research in this area has two broad orientations, product-oriented and process-oriented. Product-oriented research focuses on the texts and language produced and it is therefore of central concern to the present work. Process-oriented research, as the name suggests, focuses on how research genres come into being. They often draw on ethnographic methods, although they may include textual analysis as well. To illustrate, a process-oriented study might investigate how novice research article writers garner support from experienced colleagues. The study might draw on an ethnographic approach in devising repeated and prolonged interviews with the novice writers to unearth the forms of collaboration used. Methods may include a prolonged period of observation to develop an in-depth understanding of the processes involved. Matzler (2020) investigated the research writing mentoring that doctoral supervisors provided to their supervisees who were preparing their very first article submission. For a detailed discussion of the use of ethnography in inquiry into academic writing, see Paltridge, Starfield and Tardy (2016).

A major product-oriented strand of inquiry has been investigation into the rhetorical structure of research genres, especially the part genres of the research article, including RA abstracts (Ahmed, 2015; Al-Khasawneh, 2017), methodology sections (Lim, 2006; 2017) and discussion sections (Basturkmen, 2009; Moyetta, 2016). Inquiry of this nature generally draws on the approach to genre analysis devised by Swales and illustrated in his (1990) approach to investigating RA introductions, which resulted in the CARS (Create a research space) model.

5.3.2 Research Article, A Contested Term

The RA is generally seen as the "most prestigious member" of the "research genre set" that includes grant proposals, conference presentations, proceedings papers and communications with journals about submissions (Belcher et al., 2016: 504). The RA is generally viewed as the "pre-eminent genre of the academy" as it is the main site for the creation of disciplinary knowledge, and because it combines research reporting and research marketing functions (Hyland, 2009: 67). RAs in top-tier journals are highly regarded because the quality of the research has been validated through the journals' rigorous peer review system and selection criteria. Given the high volume of articles typically submitted to high-impact journals, rejection rates can be very high (over 90 per cent) in some journals and so only very few submissions see the light of day as a published article and as the outcome of a "prolonged and often tortuous" writing and peer-review process that can involve multiple drafts and rounds of revision in response to reviewers' comments (Hyland, 2009: 68).

The RA is certainly the pre-eminent genre in EAP research into academic writing. Surprisingly, the notion of what constitutes an RA has been subject to limited scrutiny and discussion, and genre researchers have tended to simply report that they selected RAs for their investigations. This is critiqued by Van Enk and Power (2017), who argue that there can be a good deal of variability in what can be considered an RA and thus what might be used as texts (data) in genre-based inquiries. Although the RA is a relatively stable genre, it is not fixed and evidence shows that RAs vary across disciplines (Hyland, 2004) and time (Gross, Harmon & Reidy, 2002). Van Enk and Power (op. cit.) argue that genre researchers should make explicit their criteria for selecting RAs and how they distinguish them from other kinds of texts found in academic journals.

> It is essential for genre researchers not to assume a priori and implicitly what defines this genre. The criteria used to identify research

articles (and indeed any genre under study) need to be identified and made explicit.

(Van Enk & Power, 2017: 9)

5.3.3 The Terrain

Charles and Pecorari (2016: 123) identify a range of written "expert genres", or "genres produced primarily by and for researchers" in a list that includes monographs (book-length treatments of a specific topic by one or more authors); edited books (book-length works on a particular topic with chapters written by different authors); RAs and surveys (state-of-the-art articles that describe research to date on a specific topic). Other research genres are book reviews, book proposals, review essays, bibliographical essays, encyclopedia entries, blogs and podcasts (Gaillet & Guglielmo, 2014), wikis and tweets (Kuteeva, 2016), and scientific letters – reports of no more than six pages that provide quick publication and succinct access to information on research in the sciences (Hyland, 2009).

Some research genres are "occluded" (Swales, 2004: 18). These are genres that are often hidden from view for early-career academics, although often highly visible to senior academics. An example of this is the grant proposal: those who read and evaluate such proposals are usually established academic professionals who make the decisions about applications and how projects are funded. Charles and Pecorari argue (2016: 127) that those who "need most to learn about how the genre is typically and successfully realised are not the ones who have the opportunity to read it."

5.3.4 Comparative Inquiry

Although much of the early EAP and ERPP genre-based research aimed primarily to produce a description of moves (rhetorical structure) in the target genre, recently many studies have had comparative aims. Comparative genre studies seek to identify how the practice of a genre may vary between different groups of writers, and they generally use frequency data or other measures of quantification to establish differences (Basturkmen, 2014). Studies have compared writers with different first-language backgrounds and writing in different languages. See, for example, Sheldon's (2019) study of discussion sections written by English L1 and L2 and Castilian Spanish L1 writers; Loi's (2010) study of research article introductions in Chinese and English; and Zanina's (2017) study of English and Russian RA abstracts in management. One major thrust of research interest has been comparison of how writers in different disciplines structure a particular genre, a topic that will be examined in detail in Chapter 6.

5.3.5 Merging Move and Corpus Analysis

Recent product-oriented research has routinely merged move analysis with corpus linguistics, very often doing so to investigate overt markers of interpersonal aspects of text, such as stance or engagement (Belcher et al., 2016: 504). Move and corpus analysis were merged in El-Dakhs's (2018) investigation of meta discourse in a study comparing abstracts in RAs and PhD theses, and in a comparative investigation of book reviews in two different linguistic and cultural settings (Sanz, 2009). Sanz compared evaluation in book reviews written in Spanish by authors at Spanish institutions and published in prestigious History journals in Spain and those written in English by authors at British institutions and published in prestigious History journals in Britain. Positive (praise) and negative (critique) evaluative remarks were identified. The study found a similar frequency of evaluative remarks in both sets of texts. However, the Spanish reviews included far fewer negative evaluations than the British reviews.

5.4 Studies in Focus

This section includes inquiries into two written genres and one spoken event. It includes genre-based studies of conference proposals and research article introductions, and a study into the kind of question-answer sessions that typically follow academic conference presentations.

5.4.1 Conference Proposals

> Halleck, G.B. & Connor, U.M. (2006). Rhetorical moves in TESOL conference proposals. *Journal of English for Academic Purposes*, 5: 70–86.

Conference proposals play an important role in the lives of academics. Not only do conference presentations serve as a key means by which academics introduce their research to their peers but also it is very often the case that funding for attendance at conferences depends upon having a paper accepted for presentation. The conference proposal is thus an "indispensable gateway" to an important type of "public platform" in the lives of academics (Halleck & Connor, 2006). Proposals are a persuasive genre as they function to convince the conference selection committee of the relevance of the proposal topic and approach, that it fits into current interests of the disciplinary community and that it is a recognizable contribution to disciplinary knowledge. They are an occluded genre in many cases as only the title of the paper and a short synopsis is published in the conference programme. The full proposal, or summary, is used in the selection process but often is not available as an example that writers preparing their own proposals can refer to.

Halleck and Connor's (2006) study was based on the analysis of 200 proposals to a TESOL (Teaching English to Speakers of other Languages) conference in North America. The study aimed to identify the rhetorical moves the writers had used in the one-page summaries of successful proposals, that is proposals accepted for inclusion in the conference programme, and any differences between successful and unsuccessful proposals in terms of moves. Additionally, it investigated possible differences in moves across three sub-genres, proposals for empirical research, teaching applications, and for discussion of teaching or administrative issues. The study drew on existing classifications of moves (Swales, 1990) and research grant proposals (Connor, 2000).

The successful proposals were found to be significantly longer than the unsuccessful proposals. However, no differences were found in relation to the types of moves used in both sets of texts. The moves in the conference proposals were found to be very similar to those in the one-page summaries at the start of research grant proposals, although one additional move was identified in the conference proposal and one move was relabelled. The new move, MEANS 2, detailed the procedures used in the presentation, and the label *outcomes* replaced the label *achievements* that had been used for grant proposals (72). Halleck and Connor (2006) present a ten-move rhetorical structure for the conference proposal genre (see Figure 5.1). The sequence of moves varied in the conference proposals. However, no move was obligatory, that is, always present. Some differences were observed in moves across the three sub-genres. For example, the *importance claim* move occurred much more frequently in teaching applications proposals than the empirical and issues proposals.

5.4.2 Question-and-Answer Sessions at the End of Conference Presentations

> Wulff, S., Swales, J.M. & Keller, K. (2009). "We have about seven minutes for questions": the discussion sessions from a specialised conference. *English for Specific Purposes*, 28: 79–92.

> TERRITORY establishes the situation in which the activity in the proposal is placed or physically located.
>
> **Reporting previous research (RPR)** refers to text that reports on or refers to earlier research in the field, either by the proposing researcher or by others.
>
> **GAP** indicates that there is a lack of knowledge or a problem in the territory. This move serves to explain the motivation of the study
>
> **GOAL** is the statement of aim, or general objective of the proposed activity.
>
> **MEANS 1** indicates the methods, procedures, plans of action, and tasks that the proposal specifies as leading to the GOAL.
>
> **MEANS 2** includes the methods and procedures to carry out the actual presentation.
>
> **OUTCOMES** describes the anticipated results, findings or achievements of the study or other proposed activity.
>
> **BENEFITS** explains the intended or projected outcomes which could be considered useful to the "real world" outside the study itself, or even outside of the research field.
>
> **IMPORTANCE CLAIM** presents the proposal, objectives, anticipated outcomes, or the territory as particularly important or topical, much needed or urgent with respect to either the "real" or research worlds.
>
> **COMPETENCE CLAIM** contains statements to the effect that the proposer is well qualified.

Figure 5.1 Rhetorical moves in TESOL conference proposals.
Source: Halleck & Connor, 2006: 73.

Conference presentations are integral to the work-life of academics (Forey & Feng, 2016), and they play important networking functions, and attending and giving presentations provide academics with "a momentary sense of belonging and community" (Hyland, 2009: 79). The conference presentation is not a one-off event, rather it is part of a sequence of events in the evolution of a research project. The conference presentation may be given while the research is still in process or at the conclusion. Academic conferences too are a sequence of events. They begin with a conference announcement and the call for papers, which is followed by submission and review of proposals, preparation and then presentation of the conference paper. It is common for academic conference presentations to conclude with a question-and-answer session in which the audience asks questions or makes comments on the presentation. This session can play an important role in a research project in providing fresh insights from the audience that the researcher may not have considered. The presenter or presenters may gain opportunities to understand how others perceive the research. What the audience found particularly interesting may suggest how best to frame the research in any future journal submissions.

Wulff, Swales and Keller (2009) analysed the question-and-answer sessions following presentations at a small, specialised conference (a genre studies conference) in a North American setting. They analysed 20 presentations from the *John Swales Conference Corpus* (JSCC). In these presentations, 20 minutes had been allotted to the presentation and ten minutes to a question-and-answer session. The average length of the sessions in the analysed recordings was around six and a half minutes.

Transcripts of the question-and-answer sessions were analysed using corpus analysis software and frequent lexical, or phraseological, patterns were identified, and these were compared to those in the presentations. This revealed the patterns shown in Table 5.1. Some patterns in the presentations served to direct the audience to visuals (e.g. *you can see here*) and to the steps in their research (e.g. *I wanted to*) whereas the most common patterns in the question-and-answer (discussion) sessions were related to evaluation, which included hedges and suggestions.

The patterns illustrated in Table 5.2 indicate that criticism in question-and-answer sessions was generally indirect. Rather than using direct expressions, such as *I disagree, I think you're wrong, your study is too limited*, audience members used expressions such as, *it would be interesting to see if* your findings apply to a wider group or, *it seems to me that you could also collect data on X*. The study also found that presenters often reacted to comments by acknowledging their validity (e.g. *that's a really good point*), before responding to the point being made.

Table 5.1 Most prominent classes of patterns in presentations vs. discussion sessions in the JSCC

Presentations	*Discussion sections*
modified nominal phrases (*one of the, some of the, in the field*)	hedges (*I think, you know, kind of/sort of*)
	positive evaluation (*that's a very X*)
attention-directing phrases (*this is, you can see here*)	negative evaluations (*it seems to me*)
	suggestions (*would be interesting, I wonder if*)
procedural phrases (*I tried, started, wanted to*)	

Source: Wulff, Swales & Keller, 2009: 81.

Table 5.2 Patterns used to initialize and react to criticism in the discussion sections of the JSCC

Initiating criticism	Reacting to criticism
I'm going to venture a rival hypothesis ok	That's a really good point
I suggest or submit that	That would be fascinating
to me	Can I just add that
It's really much more	Thanks for bringing this up
What we're looking at	Thank you
I (just) wonder if	That's a very good question
I was just going to ask you	
I just wanted to say	
Can I make a comment?	
It seems to me	
It would be interesting	
It occurred to me	

Source: Wulff, Swales & Keller, 2009: 82.

Formulaic expressions used by the chair were identified. Typically, chairs would open and close the question-answer session with expressions, such as *"we have seven minutes for questions"* (79) and use hedging to play down that the chairs had a controlling role, for example, *"maybe* on that note it's a good place to stop" or, "we *probably* need to wrap it up" (84).

5.4.3 Evaluation Strategies in Research Article Introductions

Xu, X. & Nesi, H. (2019). Evaluation in research article introductions: A comparison of the strategies used by Chinese and British authors. *Text and Talk*, 39(6): 797–818.

RA introductions are a challenging section to write. The introductions need to present convincing arguments about the importance of their research field and the need for the current study. Xu and Nesi (2019a) analysed introductions in a corpus of RAs published in international Anglophone journals in applied linguistics. The RAs had been written by two groups of writers – Mandarin-speaking scholars educated in China or Taiwan and Anglophone scholars educated in Britain. The study sought to identify differences between the two groups in terms of the evaluative styles they used in their arguments for the centrality of the research field and the need for the current research with the overall objective of understanding cultural variation in attitude-taking in RA

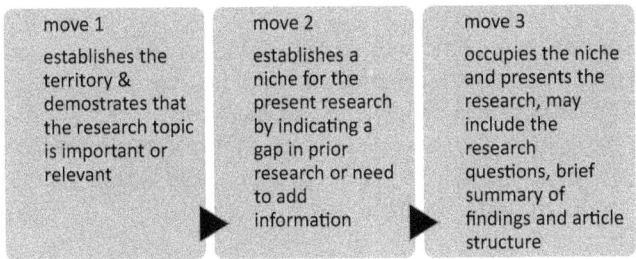

Figure 5.2 Moves in RA introductions.
Source: Based on Swales (1990: 141).

writing. Previous research had compared the moves in RA introductions by Chinese and Anglophone writers (e.g. Loi, 2010) and the linguistic choices made by these groups in writing RAs (e.g. Xu & Nesi, 2019b). Xu and Nesi (2019a) bring together both strands of research in an investigation of evaluation strategies used by the two groups in specific moves in introductions.

The analysis drew on Swales's *CARS* (create a research space) model of RA introductions. This model encapsulates the functions introductions play in expressing "the need to re-establish in the eyes of the discourse community the significance of the research field; the need to 'situate' the actual research in terms of its significance; and the need to show how this niche in the wider ecosystem will be occupied and defended." (Swales, 1990: 142). The model comprises three moves. See Figure 5.2.

Corpus analysis software was then used to search for linguistics means the writers had used to convey evaluations in the moves. To identify and classify evaluations, the study drew on a three-part framework of appraisal (Martin & White, 2005). The framework presents three areas of appraisal (engagement, attitude and graduation). Instances where the writers presented, reviewed and evaluated claims were classified as engagement, those where they expressed emotions and judgements were classified as attitude and those where they scaled up or down the strength of an evaluation were classified as graduation. The study identified statistically significant differences between the two groups of writers to reveal each groups' distinctive evaluation strategies. Some of differences in relation to specific moves are shown below.

Move 1: Establishing the territory

- British writers were more likely than the Chinese writers to refer to alternative points of view in the literature and position the present research as part of a dialogue in that literature
- Chinese writers were more likely to use multiple references to the literature to show alignment of the present study with prior research and to add authority to their claims

Move 2: Establishing the niche

- Chinese writers were more likely than the British writers to use multiple references to the literature to convey an impression that the current state of knowledge on the research topic was inadequate (see Example 1 below)
- British writers were more likely to convey an impression of personal motivation toward the research topic (see Example 2 below)

Move 3: Announcing the research

- Chinese writers were more likely than the British writers to down-scale the present study (e.g. *in our study we will **attempt** to prove that*)
- British writers were more likely to explicitly and negatively evaluate the research niche that the present research aimed to fill (e.g. *Given this **clear gap** in knowledge, the primary objective of the present study was*)

> Example 1
>
> Language anxiety always poses problems to SL/FL learners by interfering with ongoing, cognitive performance (e.g. Eysenck, 1979; MacIntyre and Gardner, 1994a; MacIntyre and Gardner, 1994b) ...
>
> Example 2
>
> Being experienced writing teachers, we believed, or perhaps wanted to believe that he was mistaken. Nonetheless, we felt compelled to investigate whether students wanted feedback, what types were preferred and what was done with it.
>
> (Examples from Xu & Nesi, 2019a: 809–810)

References

Ahmed, S. (2015). Rhetorical organisation of tourism research article abstracts. *Procedia-Social & Behavioural Sciences*, 208: 269–281.

Al-Khasawneh, F.M. (2017). A genre analysis of research article abstracts written by native and non-native speakers of English. *Journal of Applied linguistics and Language Research*, 4(1): 1–13.

Basturkmen, H. (2009). Commenting on results in published research articles and masters dissertations in language teaching, *Journal of English for Academic Purposes*, 8(4): 241–251.

Basturkmen, H. (2014). Replication research in comparative genre analysis in English for academic purposes. *Language Teaching*, 47(3): 377–386.

Belcher, D., Serrano, F.J.B. & Yang, H.S. (2016). English for professional academic purposes. In K. Hyland & P. Shaw (Eds), *The Routledge handbook of English for academic purposes* (pp. 502–514). London: Routledge.

Charles, M. & Pecorari. D. (2016). *Introducing English for academic purposes*. London: Routledge.

Connor, U. (2000). Variation in rhetorical moves in grant proposals of US humanists and scientists. *Text*, 20(1): 1–28.

El-Dakhs, D.A.S. (2018). Why are abstracts in PhD theses and research articles different? A genre-specific perspective. *Journal of English for Academic Purposes*, 36: 48–60.

Flowerdew, J. (2013). English for research publication purposes. In B. Paltridge & S. Starfield (Eds), *The handbook of English for specific purposes* (pp. 301–321). Oxford: Wiley-Blackwell.

Flowerdew, J. (2019). Power in English for academic purposes. In K. Hyland & L.L.C. Wong (Eds), *Specialised English: New directions in ESP and EAP research and practice* (pp. 50–62). Abingdon, Oxon: Routledge.

Forey, G. & Feng, D. (2016). Interpersonal meaning and audience engagement in academic presentations. In K. Hyland & P. Shaw (Eds), *The Routledge handbook of English for academic purposes* (pp. 416–430). Abingdon, Oxon: Routledge.

Gaillet, L.L. & Guglielmo, L. (2014). *Scholarly publication in a changing landscape: models for success*. Palgrave Macmillan.

Gross, A.G. Harmon, J.E. & Reidy, M.S. (2002). *Communicating science: The scientific article from the 17th century to the present*. Oxford: Oxford University Press.

Halleck, G.B. & Connor, U.M. (2006). Rhetorical moves in TESOL conference proposals. *Journal of English for Academic Purposes*, 5: 70–86.

Hyland, K. (2004). *Disciplinary discourses: Social interactions in academic writing*. Ann Arbor: University of Michigan Press.

Hyland, K. (2009). *Academic discourse: English in a global context*. London: Continuum.

Kachru, B. (1982). *The other tongue: English across cultures*. Champaign, IL: University of Illinois Press.

Koutsantoni, D. (2006). Rhetorical strategies in engineering research articles and research theses: Advanced academic literacy and relations of power. *Journal of English for Academic Purposes*, 5(1): 19–36.

Koutsantoni, D. (2009). Persuading sponsors and securing funding: Rhetorical patterns in grant proposals. In M. Charles, D. Pecorai & S. Hunston (Eds), *Academic writing: At the interface of corpus and discourse* (pp. 37–57). London: Continuum.

Kuteeva, M. (2016). Research blogs, wikis and tweets. In K. Hyland & P. Shaw (Eds), *The Routledge handbook of English for academic purposes* (pp. 431–443). Abingdon, Oxon: Routledge.

Kwase, T. (2015). Metadiscourse in the introductions of PhD theses and research articles. *Journal of English for Academic Purposes*, 20: 114–124.

Lim, J.M.H. (2006). Method sections of management research: A pedagogically motivated, qualitative study. *English for Specific Purposes*, 25(3): 282–309.

Lim, J.M.H (2017). Writing descriptions of experimental procedures in language education: Implications for the teaching of English for academic purposes. *English for Specific Purposes*, 47: 61–80.

Loi, C.K. (2010). Research article introductions in Chinese and English: A comparative genre-based study. *Journal of English for Academic Purposes*, 9: 267–279.

Martin, J.R. & White, R.R. (2005). *The language of evaluation: Appraisal in English*. Basingstoke: Palgrave Macmillan,

Matzler, P. (2020). *Doctoral writing in the natural sciences: The texts and contexts of mentoring by co-authorship*. University of Auckland, doctoral dissertation.

Moyetta, D. (2016). The discussion section of English and Spanish research articles in psychology: A contrastive study. *ESP Today*, 4(1): 87–106.

Paltridge, B., Starfield, S. & Tardy, C.M. (2016). *Ethnographic perspectives on academic writing*. Oxford: Oxford University Press.

Pérez-Llantada, C. (2012). *Scientific discourse and the rhetoric on globalisation*. New York: Continuum.

Sanz, R.L. (2009). (Non-) critical voices in the reviewing of history discourse: A cross cultural study of evaluation. In Hyland, K. & Diani, G. (Eds), *Academic evaluation* (pp. 143–160). New York: Palgrave Macmillan.

Sheldon, E. (2019). Knowledge construction of discussion/conclusion sections of research articles written by English L1 and L2 and Castilian Spanish L1 writers. *Journal of English for Academic Purposes*, 37: 1–10.

Swales, J. (1990). *Genre analysis: English in academic and research settings*. New York: Cambridge University Press.

Swales, J. (2004). *Research genres: English in academic and research settings*. Cambridge: Cambridge University Press.

Van Enk, A. & Power, K. (2017). What is a research article? Genre variability and data selection in genre research. *Journal of English for Academic Purposes*, 29: 1–11.

Wulff, S., Swales, J.M. & Keller, K. (2009). "We have about seven minutes for questions": The discussion sessions from a specialised conference. *English for Specific Purposes*, 28: 79–92.

Xu, X. & Nesi, H. (2019a). Evaluation in research article introductions: A comparison of the strategies used by Chinese and British authors. *Text and Talk*, 39(6): 797–818.

Xu, X. & Nesi, H (2019b). Differences in engagement: A comparison of the strategies used by British and Chinese research article writers. *Journal of English for Academic Purposes*, 38: 121–134.

Zanina, E. (2017). Move structure of research article abstracts on management: Contrastive study (the case of English and Russian). *Journal of Language and Education*, 3(2): 63–72.

6 Disciplinary Variation

6.1 Introduction

As discussed in Chapter 3, one major thrust of EAP linguistic inquiry has been the endeavour to identify general features of academic English, that is, features that are common across disciplines. The present chapter focuses on linguistic inquiry that has strived to identify differences in how English is used in academic disciplines, differences that are then argued to reflect the disciplinary values, ways of seeing the world and research traditions. For example, we might discover fewer language expressions that convey conjecture and possibility in writing in the hard sciences as opposed to in the social sciences. Based on this finding, we could argue that the language of conjecture and possibility is more characteristic in the social sciences, a disciplinary area where alternative research paradigms and interpretations are routinely embedded in epistemological and ontological outlooks. The positivist research paradigm is widely accepted in the hard sciences, and this can be argued to somewhat obviate the need to proffer the kind of alternative interpretations and possible explanations of findings that would call for linguistic expression of conjecture. In physical science, knowledge can be viewed as "proceeding from laboratory activities" rather than as emerging from reasoning and interpretation, as in the humanities and social sciences (Hyland, 1999: 352–353). Researchers in physical science tend more to view their research as emanating from an established theoretical framework, and the reason for some results can be obvious. (Basturkmen, 2012).

Disciplinary variation is not a new topic in EAP, and some relatively early examples of studies on the topic can be found. However, some early studies (e.g. Holmes, 1997) aimed to identify commonalities and, based on evidence of commonalities across disciplines, provide a description of an academic genre or event. By contrast, the studies examined in the present chapter aim to identify distinctive features of a discipline's practice of a genre or of the use of academic English. A genre, such as the research-article discussion section, may be found to vary significantly across two or more disciplines, with the implication that novice writers in those disciplines would be better advised to examine examples and descriptions of discussion sections based on evidence from their discipline rather than from a generic description of discussion sections.

A leading light in this line of inquiry is the work of Ken Hyland, who brought the topic of disciplinary variation to the forefront in the EAP community in the last two decades. Hyland (2002) discusses conceptual notions that underlie a disciplinary orientation in EAP. In this work, Hyland argues that academic English, rather than being construed as a single, homogenous entity, should be understood as a conglomeration of subject-specific discourses, and that generic terms, such as academic English or even English for science, disguise significant variations that inquiry has established as existing between disciplinary discourses.

The present chapter discusses studies that have investigated such variations between disciplinary discourses and genres practices, and between disciplinary areas, such as hard sciences or social sciences. The reader should note, that the term *discourses* is used in this chapter rather than *discourse*, to highlight the conceptualisation of academic English as a set of varieties, and the view that disciplines each have a set of English-language practices that can be explained in relation to the discipline's ways of thinking about research and the nature of knowledge. Studies examined in this chapter have been based primarily on analysis of disciplinary texts. The selection does not include studies that have drawn in large part on other forms of data, such as interviews (Kaufhold & McGrath, 2019). It is, however, recognised that data other than texts can provide useful insights into a disciplinary community's language practices. At the same time, studies have been included in which disciplinary community members' views or explanations of their language practices have been elicited through interviews or other measures in support of a primarily text analysis inquiry.

6.2 Importance of Inquiry

The terms "disciplinarity" or "discipline-specificity" (Costley & Flowerdew, 2017: 2), are used in EAP to refer to discourse, or language use, in a particular academic discipline, such as Physics, Sociology, History or Finance. It is recognised that each discipline has its own culture, and members of it have shared beliefs, values, goals, practices, and conventions for creating and communicating disciplinary knowledge. Members, regardless of institutional or national boundaries, constitute a *community of practice* (Lave & Wenger, 1991), with common interests in sharing information and developing knowledge in their field. Each discipline has its own ways of creating and communicating knowledge and evaluating what is of value in the field.

> Each subject discipline constitutes a way of making sense of human experience that has evolved over generations and each is dependent on its own practices in instrumental processes, its criteria for judging relevance and validity, and its conventions of acceptable forms of argument. In a word, each has developed its own discourse. To work in a discipline, therefore, it is necessary to be able to engage in these practices and, in particular, to participate in the discourse of that community.
>
> (Wells, 1992, 290)

Through their scholarly work, members of a discipline draw on discourse for purposes and in ways that reflect the recognised research orientations and means of knowledge creation of their discipline. Their discourse reproduces and legitimises what is seen as valid and relevant in their discipline. The production of discourse is an important means by which a discipline's outlook is represented and generated. To inquire into disciplinary variation is, therefore, to inquire into a discipline's culture. Disciplinary discourse is an artefact of the disciplinary culture. The concept of duality of structure has been proposed in genre theory to explain that when people draw on genre rules to engage in activities in professional and institutional settings, they both constitute and simultaneously reproduce the social fabric of that setting (Berkenkotter & Huckin, 1993).

Comparative studies are not the only way to develop descriptions of a discipline's discourse. We can of course, just describe discourse in a discipline. The reader will have seen many such studies in previous chapters, for example, in Chapter 4 the studies of interaction in discussion classes on a business studies programme (Basturkmen, 2003) and, in Chapter 5, of conference proposals in language teaching (Halleck & Connor, 2006). Such studies can be considered as discipline-specific in that the linguistic data were drawn from one discipline. Researchers of such studies do not claim that their findings can be generalised to other disciplines, although they may suggest further research into whether the descriptions they derived from their investigations can in fact be applied to other disciplines. EAP linguistic enquiry into the discourse of a discipline has a long history. Bloor and Bloor (1993) investigated the ways economists modified claims in their writing, and Tarone and colleagues (1981) investigated the use of passives in astrophysics research articles.

Evidence of variation, such as disciplinary differences in the practice of a genre or the functions of a linguistic feature, bolster support for the theoretical view of academic English as a conglomeration of disciplinary discourses and counter evidence to support ideas that academic English is a homogeneous entity. This theoretical view has ramifications for teaching and learning academic English, especially proposals for teaching general academic English (EGAP). The generic version of academic English on offer is arguably a made-up abstraction rather than a real-world entity. EAP teaching has taken this on board, and ESAP instruction, where classes for learners from one discipline are provided with instruction targeting disciplinary discourse and genre practices (e.g., the types of essays students are required to produce in the discipline), has been promoted.

Hyland (2006) identifies three major orientations in teaching EAP – the skills, socialisation and academic literacies approaches. The skills approach historically has been the default approach in teaching English for study purposes. It is compatible for teaching classes of students from mixed disciplines (English for general academic purposes or EGAP). In this orientation, teaching focuses on a set of generic skills, such as referencing, note taking and essay writing, that are considered widely used across higher education. Teaching draws topics and source reading texts from general interest areas, such as layman's psychology or the environment, which are accessible to all class members. It is expected that, in the EGAP class setting, students will be able to transfer the skills and knowledge they learn to their future reading, speaking, listening and writing in their discipline. The extent to which the skills learnt in the general setting are applied or are applicable to the disciplinary setting has not been subject to much scrutiny and empirical investigation, however.

The socialisation approach focuses on orienting learners to the genres, norms and practices of specific disciplines, familiarising them with the ways the discipline constructs knowledge and what it values in writing and communication. It aims to help students access and gain the means to participate in their discipline by adjusting their discourse (how they use the language) to the norms and expectations of those disciplines. The approach is compatible with English for specific academic purposes or ESAP situations in which classes consist of students from one or a limited number of disciplines. It may sometimes be possible to incorporate a focus on discipline-specific discourse within EGAP instruction. This is illustrated in Matheson & Basturkmen (2015), which describes how some discipline-specific materials and activities were integrated into instruction on "general" academic essay writing.

The academic literacies approach focuses on assisting learners to engage in, understand and critique the discourse practices and epistemologies of their field. This approach helps students recognise the complexity and specificity of those fields, and that there is diversity in academic discourses (For teaching and learning activities, see Johns, 1997). The academic socialisation approach assumes learners need to learn the norms and conventions of their new academic discipline or culture. An academic literacies approach suggests that attempting to mimic disciplinary approved forms of discourse can lead to serious problems for many students. As learners are required to use language in unfamiliar ways, their choices of expression can become restricted and their own opinions, experiences and identities devalued (Hyland, 2006).

Findings from studies of expert disciplinary writing can play an important role in elucidating genre practices, values and expectations for the disciplinary writing or speaking of a discipline. Thus, they are of key importance to teachers and learners in ESAP settings. They are also of importance to novice academics in a discipline. Seasoned academics may have tacit knowledge of genre practices in their specialist field, but these practices may not be obvious to novice writers. The tacit knowledge of senior colleagues cannot easily be transposed into the kind of declarative knowledge that can be explained to less-experienced colleagues (see Chapter 2 for discussion of explicit and implicit knowledge). Novice disciplinary writers of research articles would likely be interested in descriptions from linguistic inquiry into research writing in their discipline. Journal editors may consider that novices to the discipline are acquiring disciplinary research practices concomitantly with disciplinary discourse practices.

Would novice academics be interested in how writing practices differ in their discipline compared to another discipline? Probably not. Description of disciplinary variation would, however, be relevant to the interests of those who provide academic writing support to faculty or junior researchers. Universities and other tertiary education providers often do provide writing retreats and research-writing seminars, or one-on-one writing support. It is important that those teaching or supporting academics in developing their writing are aware of disciplinary differences in discourse and genre practices. Generic descriptions of research writing or the research article will likely fail to reflect practices in the disciplines of attendees at their workshops or in their consultations.

6.3 Nature of Inquiry

It is generally acknowledged that discourse varies across disciplines and that disciplinary uses of language need to be understood in relation to the shared values and practices of the disciplinary culture. Hyland and Hamp-Lyons's (2002: 5–6) editorial of the first issue of the *Journal of English for Academic Purposes* referred to the "fact of discourse specificity" and the concomitant need to challenge generally-held assumptions that academic conventions are "universal and independent of particular disciplines."

As described above, genre practices in specific disciplines has been a major line of EAP inquiry, with studies describing expert genres (Lim, 2006; 2017; Oztürk, 2007) or student genres, such as Flowerdew and Forest's (2009) study of literature reviews in doctoral theses in applied linguistics. Inquiry has examined related expert and student genres (Basturkmen, 2009) and unearthed new genres, or genres, not seen in the practice of (many) other disciplines, such as Dressen-Hammouda's (2003) study of *field accounts* in research articles in geology.

What is distinctive in the discourse of a discipline, in other words, what is and is not discipline-specific, becomes apparent when the discipline's discourse is compared to that of another discipline. We may observe, for example, that some of the linguistic features we observed in the writing of the first discipline were not used as frequently in the second discipline. Or, we may observe that the linguistic features were used in the second disciplines but for different functions compared to those we observed in the discourse of the first disciplines. Or, we might observe that some linguistic features or patterns were included in the second discipline's discourse significantly more or less often than in the discourse of the first discipline. It may become apparent that the second discipline follows different conventions in their practice of a genre or that they use varying forms of argumentation. It is through comparison that we come to notice differences and thus come to understand what is discipline-specific.

Comparative genre analysis (Basturkmen, 2014) investigates similarities and differences in the practice of a genre in different disciplines. One early study of this nature was Holmes's (1997) examination of *discussion* sections in research articles in three social sciences, a study which brought to light the particularly distinctive nature of discussion in the history articles. Lim's study (2010) compared the ways results were commented on in research in education and applied linguistics. One line of inquiry is investigation into whether a genre description based on analysis of texts from one discipline can be applied to a second discipline (Basturkmen, 2012). Studies investigating genre variation in related disciplines or in sub- specialisms (Samraj, 2002; Kanoksilapatham, 2015; Kwan, Chan & Lam, 2012) have found variation. Some studies of research article organisation have been cross disciplinary, that is, they investigated research articles from a broad range of disciplines (Cotos, Huffman, & Link, 2017; Peacock, 2002). Lin and Evans (2012: 150) investigated whether the "standard" Introduction-Method-Result-Discussion (IMRD) pattern was evident in research articles from nearly 40 disciplines.

Inquiry into student writing has focused on a single discipline or compared writing in disciplines. Flowerdew and Forest (2009) examined literature reviews in doctoral theses in applied linguistics. Disciplinary variation in assessed genres of student writing was the topic of a large-scale study in UK universities (Gardner & Nesi, 2012). The book *Genres across Disciplines: Student Writing* presents a classification of thirteen genre families (groups of similar texts). Although the genres were seen in one form or another across many disciplines, genre practices varied – see the description of this study in Chapter 4.4.1. *Case reports,* a key learning genre in business studies, have been found to vary in structure and style in relation to business sub-specialism (Nathan, 2013). Bruce (2010) investigated differences in *essay* assignments in Sociology and English.

Corpus analysis has been used in comparative studies to identify the incidence and use of specific linguistic features. A suite of studies investigated differences in the use of reporting clauses in citations (Charles, 2006), noun + that patterns (Charles, 2007) and *adverbials of result* (Charles, 2011) in thesis writing in politics compared to materials science. Expressions of evaluation and stance signalled by that + complement clause structures in research articles in business studies and medicine were investigated in one recent study (Kim & Crosthwaite, 2019). The study found a significantly higher incidence of the structure in the business studies compared to the medical articles and this finding led the researchers to suggest that business writing has a more explicitly evaluative and interpersonally engaged style than medicine. Corpus analysis has been used to identify frequently or distinctively used vocabulary in disciplines. Wang, Liang and Ge (2008) report their corpus-based investigation of vocabulary in medical research articles, which led to development of the *Medical Academic Word List.*

Inquiry into the possibility of disciplinary variation has generally shown evidence of such variation. However, a finding of disciplinary variation is not inevitable. Chang (2012) searched for differences in the use of questions by professors in classroom teaching in three disciplinary groupings (Humanities and Arts, Social Sciences and Education and Physical Sciences and Engineering). Analysis of the professors' question forms and functions largely revealed similarities across the three groupings. Chang concluded that "for questions in academic lectures at the tertiary level, the influence of genre seems to outweigh that of disciplinary culture" (op. cit. p. 103). A review of research into spoken academic genres led Swales (2004) to conclude that the kind of disciplinary differences reported for academic writing were less evident in academic speaking, and that academic speaking is more homogeneous than academic writing. However, findings from a recent study (Hu & Liu, 2018), in the *Studies in Focus* section below, appear to provide some evidence of disciplinary variation in speaking.

6.4 Studies in Focus

6.4.1 Three-minute Thesis Presentations

Hu, G. & Liu, Y. (2018). Three-minute thesis presentations as an academic genre: A cross-disciplinary study of genre moves. *Journal of English for Academic Purposes*, 35: 16–30.

Many academic genres are well-established and familiar. One recently emerging genre is the three-minute (3MT) thesis presentation of graduate students. This is a genre that has appeared around the world, often in competition-style events. In these presentations, graduate students submit a synopsis of their research to a disciplinary mixed audience. There are usually guidelines, such as the requirement that they use only one power-point slide. The genre serves an important educative function in helping students consider how to communicate with a non-specialist audience, as well as preparing them to explain their research to a specialist audience in the PhD oral defence. Hu and Liu (2018) drew on the approach to genre analysis developed by Swales (1990; 2004) to analyse the rhetorical structure of over 140 video-recorded three-minute thesis presentations by PhD students, which they sourced from the public domain, such as from YouTube. The presentations were classified into disciplinary fields following Becher (1989), and a two-way comparison was made between hard (Biological Sciences and Mechanical Engineering) and soft (Education and History) disciplines on the one hand, and between pure (Biological Sciences and History) and applied (Mechanical Engineering and Education) disciplines on the other hand. An analysis of moves was made. The analysis revealed a schematic structure of six obligatory moves (*orientation*, *rationale*, *purposes*, *methods*, *implication* and *termination*) and two optional moves (*framework and results*). Obligatory moves occurred in 80 per cent or more of the presentations, and optional moves occurred in fewer than 80 per cent of the samples.

Table 6.1 Moves more or less likely to occur in three-minute thesis presentations by disciplinary groupings

Group	Framework Move	Methods Move	Group	Results Move
Hard disciplines	Less likely	More likely	Pure disciplines	More likely
Soft disciplines	More likely	Less likely	Applied disciplines	Less likely

Source: Based on Hu and Liu (2018: 27).

Presentations in all disciplinary groupings were similar in that they included most of the moves. Nevertheless, some statistically significant differences were seen in *framework, methods* and *results* moves (see Table 6.1). These differences are explained in relation to differences in the dominant research paradigms of the disciplines. Presenting a theoretical *framework* as the background for a study was more evident in the soft disciplines, where there is not always a commonly agreed framework for research or approach to investigation of the topic. The *methods* move was more frequent in the hard disciplines, where there is a greater emphasis on describing and justifying research methods and procedures. Presenters in the pure sciences were more likely to include a *results* move, since research in this area is largely concerned with "creating, explaining and interpreting knowledge" compared to presenters in applied disciplines, where research has a primary "orientation towards knowledge application" (Hu & Liu, 2018: 27).

6.4.2 Changing Patterns of Disciplinary Meta Discourse

Hyland, K. & Jiang, F. K. (2018). "In this paper we suggest"; Changing patterns of disciplinary metadiscourse. *English for Specific Purposes*, 51: 18–30.

Most studies described in this book have investigated academic language use at a certain point of time. However, it is important to realise that academic English is not fixed and unchanging, but rather mutating and developing over time. Hyland and Jiang's study (2018) highlights the need to recognise the "significant changes in the apparently frozen surfaces of (usually) scientific research articles" (18). An earlier study (Hyland & Jiang, 2017) had put to the test the common assertion that academic writing has become more informal in recent times. The study had found evidence that academic writing in the hard sciences was becoming more informal, although writing in social sciences was in fact becoming more formal.

To explore the topic of disciplinary differences in the development of academic writing, Hyland and Jiang (2018) examined differences in the use of meta discourse. Meta discourse was defined as writers' commentary on the text they produce which makes explicit how they intend messages to be understood. They drew on a large corpus of research articles published over a fifty-year period with reference to three points in time (1965, 1985 and 2015). The study investigated the incidence of meta discourse markers across two soft sciences (Applied Linguistics and Sociology) and two hard sciences (Biology and Engineering), drawing on the existing two-part classification, *interactive* and *interactional*, resources of meta discourse (Hyland, 2005). As shown in Figure 6.1, *interactive resources* are linguistic devices that guide the reader through the text, and *interactional resources* are devices that signal the writer's personal point of view or that engage readers directly in the text.

Corpus analysis was used to identify the meta discourse resources in the texts, and manual checks were made to confirm that each electronically identified resource did indeed function in the text as meta discourse. Log likelihood measures (a form of inferential statistics used in corpus analysis) were used to identify significant differences and changes.

Interactive resources guide readers through writing content
Transitions: signal relationships between content – e.g. *as well as, therefore*
Frame markers: signal writing structure or goals – e.g. *firstly, this paper aims to*
Endophoric markers: link content to other text parts – e.g. *see Table 2, as argued above*
Evidentials: identify sources outside the text – e.g. *Fu (2020) describes, reports show*
Code glosses: reformulate content – e.g. *to illustrate, in other words*
Interactional resources address writer/reader concerns and signal writers' identity projection
Hedges: withhold complete commitment to content – e.g. *possible, may, could, seems*
Boosters: convey certainty and strengthen claims – e.g. *indeed, clearly*
Attitude markers: express writer view of ideas – e.g. *surprise, agreement*
Engagement markers: address and engage readers – e.g. *you (second person pronouns), have you considered (questions), please note that (imperatives)*
Self-mentions: refer directly to the author(s) – e.g. *I, our work*

Source: Based on Hyland Hyland & Jiang (2018: 20).

Figure 6.1 Classification of interactive and interactional meta discourse

The study found that a major increase (11.5%) in the frequency of meta discourse use over the fifty-year period which was due largely to the significant increase in interactive resources. There were very large increases in *evidentials* (citations) and *code glosses* (e.g., explanations of terms), which the researchers explained with reference to the wider dissemination of research publications and growing complexity of research over time.

There was a significant decrease in the use of *interactional* resources, although *hedges* remained the most commonly used type of interactional marker across the entire period. There were large decreases in the use of *boosters* and *attitude markers*, which seemed to suggest a change and a move away from authors projecting a "strong authorial standpoint on issues" (22). There was, however, a substantial increase in *self-mentions*, which seemed to suggest that professional academic writers were becoming increasingly assertive in signalling their presence in the research and garnering recognition for claims.

Interactive resources increased similarly across the four disciplines. However, different patterns were observed in *interactional resources*, especially in the use of markers of author stance, or standpoint (*boosters* and *attitude markers*). Substantial declines were seen in the use of interactional resources in the soft sciences, but an overall increase was seen in the hard sciences, which the researcher argue may reflect the cultures of the disciplines and their views on "how best to represent their work, their readers and themselves" (28).

6.4.3 Discipline-specific Phrase Lists for Secondary School

Green, C. & Lambert, J. (2019). Position vectors, homologous chromosomes and gamma rays: Promoting disciplinary literacy through Secondary Phrase Lists. *English for Specific Purposes*, 53: 1–12.

From around middle school, the texts used at school become technical and specialised enough to warrant a disciplinary approach. At this point, students need to start acquiring the specialised language patterns of the subjects, or disciplines, they take at school. Learning discipline-specific vocabulary, including disciplinary ways of using vocabulary, is an essential part of developing disciplinary literacy. Content words (e.g., *rays*) and patterns in the way content words are used, or phrases (e.g., *gamma rays*), encapsulate concepts in a discipline. As well as knowing single unit disciplinary words (e.g., *rays*), students need to learn content word patterns to access and express conceptual knowledge in their school subjects. This is the same for native and non-native speakers of English as they are all learning a specialised register of English for the first time. Word lists of single unit disciplinary vocabulary can omit much of the vocabulary that is critical for developing conceptual understanding in a discipline (Green & Lambert, 2019).

Green and Lambert collected a corpus of over two hundred, English-language secondary school textbooks representing eight subjects, most of which were on lists of recommended reading for year levels 9–12 in Singapore. Using corpus linguistics, frequently co-occurring two-word units (noun-noun, noun-verb, adjective-noun, noun-verb and verb-adverb) patterns were identified. Measures were taken to ensure that the patterns were meaningful and pedagogically useful, including the kind of *Mutual Information* (MI) measure and teacher ratings measures described in Chapter 3.4.4.3. Phrases that met the stringent criteria used in the analysis were used, (1) to develop the *Secondary Phrase Lists* (SPL) for eight school subjects (Mathematics, Biology, Chemistry, Physics, English, History, Geography and Economics) and (2) to assess the extent of variation in the phrases across the disciplines. Table 6.2 shows the most frequent verb-noun phrases by discipline.

Table 6.2 Most frequent adjective-noun phrases

	Biology	Mathematics	Chemistry	Physics
1	active transport	straight line	hydrochloric acid	magnetic field
2	nervous system	standard deviation	sulfuric acid	kinetic energy
3	active site	significant figures	periodic table	potential difference
4	small intestine	shaded region	boiling point	electric field
5	spinal cord	decimal places	ethanoic acid	potential energy
6	homologous chromosomes	quadratic equation	boiling points	thermal energy
7	fatty acids	stationary points	molecular formula	resultant force
8	aerobic respiration	stationary point	molecular mass	gravitational field
9	natural selection	minimum point	nitric acid	time graph
10	living organisms	simultaneous equations	aqueous solution	electrical energy

	Economics	Geography	History	English
1	United States	urban areas	Soviet Union	English language
2	aggregate demand	rural areas	United States	young people
3	economic growth	economic development	Cold War	other people
4	total cost	tropical storms	eastern Europe	different types
5	real GDP	local people	communist party	key words
6	aggregate supply	developed countries	foreign policy	human beings
7	total revenue	other countries	Korean War	short story
8	marginal cost	economic growth	civil war	standard English
9	monetary policy	tropical rainforest	Southeast Asia	main idea
10	short run	different types	Prime Minister	different ways

Source: Green & Lambert, 2019: 8.

Only eight phrases were found to occur across all the disciplines and only 2 per cent of the phrases occurred in more than half the disciplines. There were more phrases in common between mathematics and the science subjects than between the humanities subjects. These results demonstrated a high level of disciplinary variation and specificity. There was little evidence of a "core lexical academic vocabulary" in terms of content word phrases (11).

References

Basturkmen, H. (2003). So what happens when the tutor walks in? Some observations on interaction in a university discussion group with and without the tutor. *Journal of English for Academic Purposes*, 2: 21–33.

Basturkmen, H. (2009). Commenting on results in published research articles and masters dissertations in Language Teaching. *Journal of English for Academic Purposes*, 8(4): 241–251.

Basturkmen, H. (2012). A genre-based investigation of the discussion section of research articles in dentistry and applied linguistics. *Journal of English for Academic Purposes*, 11(2): 134–144.

Basturkmen, H. (2014). Replication research in comparative genre analysis in English for academic purposes. *Language Teaching*, 47: 377–386.

Becher, T. (1989). *Academic tribes and territories: Intellectual enquiry and the culture of disciplines*. Buckingham: SHRE and the Open University Press.

Berkenkotter, C. & Huckin, T.N. (1993). Rethinking genre from a socio-cognitive perspective. *Written Communication*, 10: 475–509.

Bloor, M. & Bloor, T. (1993). How economists modify propositions. In W. Henderson, T. Dudley-Evans & R. Blackhouse (Eds). *Economics and language* (pp. 153–169). London: Routledge.

Bruce, I. (2010). Textual and discoursal resources used in the essay genre in sociology and English. *Journal of English for Academic Purposes*, 9(3): 153–166.

Chang, Y-Y. (2012). The use of questions by professors in lectures given in English: Influences of disciplinary cultures. *English for Specific Purposes*, 31: 103–116.

Charles, M. (2006). Phraseological patterns in reporting clauses used in citation: A corpus-based study of theses in two disciplines. *English for Specific Purposes*, 25: 310–331.

Charles, M (2007). Argument or evidence? Disciplinary variation in the use of the *Noun* that pattern in stance construction. *English for Specific Purposes*, 26: 203–218.

Charles, M. (2011). Adverbials of result: Phraseology and functions in the Problem–Solution pattern. *Journal of English for Academic Purposes*, 10, 1: 47–60.

Costley, T. & Flowerdew, J. (2017). Introduction. In Flowerdew, J. & Costley, T. (Eds.) *Discipline-specific writing: Theory into practice* (pp. 1–11). Abingdon, Oxon: Routledge.

Cotos, E., Huffman, S. & Link, S. (2017). A move/step model for methods sections: demonstrating rigour and credibility. *English for Specific Purposes*, 46: 90–106.

Dressen-Hammouda, D. (2003). Geologists' implicit persuasive strategies and the construction of evaluative evidence. *Journal of English for Academic Purposes*, 2(4): 273–290.

Flowerdew, J. & Forest, R.W. (2009). Schematic structure and lexico-grammatical realization in corpus-based genre analysis: The case of research in the PhD literature review. In M. Charles, D. Pecorari & S. Hunston (Eds), *Academic writing: At the interface of corpus and discourse* (pp. 15–36). London: Equinox.

Gardner, S. & Nesi, H. (2012). A classification of genre families in university student writing. *Applied Linguistics*, 34(1): 1–29.

Green, C. & Lambert, J. (2019). Position vectors, homologous chromosomes and gamma rays: Promoting disciplinary literacy through Secondary Phrase Lists. *English for Specific Purposes*, 53: 1–12.

Halleck, G.B. & Connor, U.M. (2006). Rhetorical moves in TESOL conference proposals. *Journal of English for Academic Purposes*, 5: 70–86.

Holmes, R. (1997). Genre analysis, and the social sciences: An investigation of the structure of research article discussion sections in three disciplines. *English for Specific Purposes*, 16(4), 321–337.

Hu, G. & Liu, Y. (2018). Three-minute thesis presentations as an academic genre: A cross disciplinary study of genre moves. *Journal of English for Academic Purposes*, 35: 16–30.

Hyland, K. (1999). Academic attribution: Citation and the construction of disciplinary knowledge. *Applied Linguistics*, 20(3): 341–367.

Hyland, K. (2005). *Metadiscourse*. London: Continuum.

Hyland, K. (2006). *English for academic purposes: An advanced resource book*. London: Routledge.

Hyland, K. & Hamp-Lyons, L. (2002). EAP: Issues and directions. *Journal of English for Academic Purposes*, 1: 1–12.

Hyland, K. & Jiang, F.K. (2017). Is academic writing becoming more informal? *English for Specific Purposes*, 45: 40–51.

Hyland, K. & Jiang, F. K. (2018). "In this paper we suggest"; Changing patterns of disciplinary metadiscourse. *English for Specific Purposes*, 51: 18–30.

Johns, A.M. (1997). *Text, role and context: Developing academic literacies*. New York: Cambridge University Press.

Kanoksilapatham, B. (2015). Distinguishing textual features characterizing structural variation in research articles across three engineering sub-discipline corpora. *English for Specific Purposes*, 37: 74–86.

Kaufhold, K. & McGrath, L. (2019). Revisiting the role of "discipline" in writing for publication in two social sciences. *Journal of English for Academic Purposes*, 40: 115–128.

Kim, C. & Crosthwaite, P. (2019). Disciplinary differences in the use of evaluative *that*: Expression of stance via that-clauses in business and medicine. *Journal of English for Academic Purposes*, 41: 10075.

Kwan, B., Chan, H. & Lam, C. (2012). Evaluating prior scholarship in literature reviews of research articles: A comparative study of practices in two research paradigms. *English for Specific Purposes* 31(3): 188–201.
Lave, J. & Wenger, E. (1991). *Situated learning: Legitimate peripheral participation*. New York: Cambridge University Press.
Lim, J.M.H. (2006). Method sections of management research articles: A pedagogically motivated qualitative study. *English for Specific Purposes*, 25(3): 282–309.
Lim, J.M.H. (2010). Commenting on results in applied linguistics and education: A comparative genre-based investigation. *Journal of English for Academic Purposes*, 9: 280–294.
Lim, J.M.H. (2017). Writing descriptions of experimental procedures in language education: Implications for the teaching of English for academic purposes. *English for Specific Purposes*, 47, 61–80.
Lin, L. & Evans, S. (2012). Structural patterns in empirical research articles: A cross-disciplinary study. *English for Specific Purposes*, 31: 150–160.
Matheson, N. & Basturkmen, H. (2015). Developing a research-informed academic writing curriculum using a text bank of student writing. In P. Shrestha (Ed.), *Current development in English for academic and specific purposes: Local innovations and global perspectives* (pp. 139–156). Reading: Garnet.
Nathan, P. (2013). Academic writing in the business school. The genre of the business case report. *Journal of English for Academic Purposes*, 12: 57–68.
Öztürk, I. (2007). The textual organisation of research article introductions in applied linguistics: Variability within a single discipline. *English for Specific Purposes*, 26(1): 25–38.
Peacock, M. (2002). Communicative moves in the discussion section of research articles. *System*, 30: 479–497.
Samraj, B. (2002). Introductions in research articles: Variations across disciplines. *English for Specific Purposes*, 21: 1–17.
Swales, J.M. (1990). *Genre analysis: English in academic and research settings*. Cambridge: Cambridge University Press.
Swales, J.M. (2004). *Research genres: Explorations and applications*. Cambridge: Cambridge University Press.
Tarone, E., Dwyer, S., Gillet, S. & Icke, V. (1981). On the use of the passive in astrophysics journal articles. *ESP Journal*, 1: 123–140.
Wang, J., Liang, S-l. & Ge, G-c. (2008). Establishment of a medical academic word list. *English for Specific Purposes*, 27: 442–458.
Wells, G. (1992). The centrality of talk in education. In Norman, K. (Ed.) *Thinking voices: The work of the national oracy project*. London: Hodder & Stoughton.

7 Conclusion and Future Directions

7.1 Introduction

Chapter 7 identifies topics where there has been a substantial body of empirical research and those where research has been limited. Topics where empirical research has been limited are suggested as directions for future research – see section 7.2. In brief, there has been considerable inquiry into research articles, study genres in university settings, the discourse of the Applied Linguistics community and studies of academic writing. By contrast, research and description of academic English in secondary school settings and of interactive spoken academic English have been limited. The Chapter sets out A *Classification Framework for Inquiry and Description of Academic English*. Categories in the *Framework* draw on topics and distinctions discussed in the chapters of the book. Suggestions are made for how readers might use the *Framework*. The chapter ends with a positive appraisal of linguistic inquiry in EAP and a suggestion for further conceptual inquiry.

7.2 Directions for Future Empirical Inquiry

There are a number of topics on which there has been considerable research inquiry and other topics where research inquiry has been limited. A recent bibliometric study of article abstracts over two time periods (1980–2000 and 2001–2020) identified changes in the most frequently examined topics in EAP research (Hyland & Jiang, in press). Comparison between the two time periods shows patterns in the topics that have been addressed in research. Academic writing, genre, discipline and interaction, higher education and graduate studies are listed amongst topics that significantly increased over the two time periods. The topic of higher education was found to be much more frequent in the research than the topic of secondary school. The reader will have seen in the book chapters reviews of a number of studies in higher-education settings. Only one inquiry in the Studies in Focus sections (Section 6.4.3) concerned academic English in secondary school. Learning academic English starts well before higher education, and there is a need for descriptions of academic English in secondary education. Yet, EAP inquiry into academic English in secondary school has been very limited to date.

The topic of graduate students appears to have attracted more research attention than undergraduate students in recent years. The frequency of graduate students as a research topic was more than double that of undergraduate students in the 2001–2020 list (Hyland & Jiang, in press). My personal observation is that there has been much research interest in recent years into graduate student writing and much less published research into undergraduate writing. Graduate student writing is an important topic and there are increasing numbers of student engaged in graduate studies. Nevertheless, many more students are engaged in undergraduate studies. In recent years, there have been noteworthy inquiries into student-assessed writing (Nesi & Gardner, 2012) and into teaching academic writing (Wingate, 2012). Further inquiry into academic English in secondary school and university undergraduate settings would be valuable.

Academic speaking and speaking skills do not appear in the lists of popular topics in Hyland and Jiang (in press) although academic writing and writing skills do. Possibly, works listed under the topic *interaction* were studies of spoken interaction. My informal observations of the EAP literature over recent decades would suggest that there have been far more publications about academic writing than academic speaking. This may be explained with reference to the importance of academic writing for students and academics. However, I suspect that a further explanation for the relatively limited research into academic speaking relates to the relative ease of collecting written texts to use as data for an inquiry. Samples of writing in the public domain, such as research articles, are fairly straightforward to collate for the purposes of research. It can be difficult, however, to collect samples of academic speaking, especially recordings of live events involving multiple participants. However, there are now corpora of academic speaking available. See, for example, the British Academic Spoken English (BASE) corpus and the Michigan Corpus of American Spoken English (MICASE). Speaking can be challenging to analyze as it does not necessarily progress in the kind of linear, predictable pathways that academic writing often does, and analysis may not lead to the kind of immediately understandable description that tends to emerge from genre-based investigation of academic writing. Further inquiry into academic spoken English is an avenue for future research, as relatively little is known. There has been a significant body of literature on lecture discourse (see Chapter 4). Lectures are often largely monologues. Other teaching genres, such as interactive classroom teaching and discussion classes, that involve dialogic or multi-party speaking, have come to play an increasingly important role in education and are topics on which further research and description is needed.

There has been a plethora of studies into research articles, especially studies of research articles in Applied Linguistics, the field with which nearly all EAP specialists are most familiar (Swales, 2019). As a result, the discourse community we know the most about is that of Applied Linguistics, and the academic genre we know most about is the research article. There seems to be an abundance of research in these areas, and possibly more researchers could turn their attention to building descriptions of discourse in other disciplines and in other genres. It is still possible to identify new genres or new variants of known genres (see, for example, Hu & Liu, 2018; Camiciottoli, 2020).

Investigating the discourse of unfamiliar disciplines can be challenging in terms of understanding texts of technical content. Swales (2019: 77) identifies rhetorical structure genre analysis as an area that has been "over-explored" in recent years especially when studies are heavily descriptive in terms of the moves and steps involved, but not very informative about how the structure can be interpreted and explained. Research that involves some form of collaboration with disciplinary specialists may be helpful in this regard. It is not always easy to obtain collaboration, not least because disciplinary specialists tend to have demanding research agendas and/or workloads. Those investigating disciplinary English may try to seek relatively undemanding forms of collaboration, such as asking the disciplinary specialist to check a description of a genre structure already drafted or to answer targeted questions about the function of a professional genre in the discipline, disciplinary forms of argumentation (Basturkmen, 2012) and disciplinary expectations for a speech event or for student writing.

In terms of linguistic forms (e.g., grammatical or lexical features, meta discourse or other text-surface type of discourse features), disciplinary experts may not be able to answer questions about why they made certain linguistic choices in writing or speaking. In using such linguistic features they may have drawn on their procedural, implicitly derived knowledge. This kind of knowledge is not necessarily accessible for explanation. They may, however, be aware of the kind of "form-function linkage(s)" described in Swales (2019: 78). See discussion of implicit and explicit knowledge in Chapter 2. The topic of the extent to which academic writers or speakers can reflect on and talk about the linguistic forms they use can be suggested as a direction for future research. It is possible that some of their linguistic choices are made strategically and with the kind of conscious attention that would be amenable to description and explanation.

Most research into study genres and events has been in university settings. At present, description of study genres and events in vocational education settings is very limited. Parkinson (2019) describes the builder's diary, a workplace genre that has been repurposed for vocational, educational objectives. Coxhead and colleagues (2019) report research in this emerging area of inquiry.

Now that a considerable body of description of the research article as a genre or as a set of part genres is available, it may be time for inquiry to move away from inquiry into research articles and towards inquiry into change and development in research writing, See, for example, Tusting et al. (2019) on how academic writing is changing as a professional academic activity. To date, most EAP inquiry into research writing has examined writing at a point in time. Resultingly, current descriptions may give the impression that academic writing is static, a kind of fixed entity. More research is needed to develop understanding of ways academic writing can change over time.

7.3 A Classification Framework

A classification scheme for EAP linguistic inquiry and description is shown in Table 7.1. The *Classification Framework for Inquiry and Description of Academic English* draws on topics and distinctions from the present work. The *Framework* aims to provide a means by which readers, as consumers of linguistic inquiry, or researchers who are planning an inquiry, can classify a study or description. For example, PhD or masters students in Applied Linguistics might find it helpful to use the *Framework* when considering how to develop a study of academic English for a dissertation or thesis.

The left of the Table lists the broad topic areas covered by the different chapters in the present book. The list is not exhaustive and other topic areas are possible. Column 1 concerns the texts used as data and whether these are written or spoken academic texts. Column 2 concerns the scope of the inquiry and whether the inquiry only includes analysis of texts or whether it includes investigation into context as well. See Chapter 2.4. Paltridge (2006: 98) describes text-first or context-first options in genre studies, saying, "We may decide to start by looking at the typical

Table 7.1 A classification framework for inquiry and description of academic English

	1 Data Written and/or spoken texts	2 Scope Text only or text & context	3. Setting e.g. school, undergraduate, postgraduate, faculty	4. Linguistic focus e.g. grammar, vocabulary, rhetorical structure, meta discourse, speech functions	5. Discipline(s)	6. Nature of description Point in time or change over time
General academic register						
Study genres & events						
Professional research genres						
Disciplinary variation						
Other						

discourse patterns in the text we are interested in, or we may decide to start with an examination of the context of the texts we want to investigate." These options can be applied to other types of linguistic inquiry, not only genre analytic studies. Column 3 can be used to classify the setting in terms of levels of education, or faculty. The linguistic focus or focuses of the inquiry can be noted in Column 4 and the discipline(s) from which the written and/or spoken texts used as data can be noted in Column 5. Finally, the reader or researcher can note in Column 6 whether the inquiry or description is of academic English at a point in time or of changes in academic English over time (developmental).

Basturkmen's (2003) study of spoken interaction in a discussion class on an MBA program (chapter 4.4.3) can be used to illustrate how the *Framework* can be used. The row "Study genres & events" is selected. As the study was an inquiry into *spoken* interaction, it was based on analysis of spoken texts (Column 1 – spoken texts). The scope was limited to analysis of texts and did not include inquiry into the context (Column 2 – text only). The setting was that of postgraduate study in a university context (Column 3 – postgraduate). The linguistic analysis focused on patterns of interaction (Column 4 – interaction patterns) and the texts were from business studies (Column 5 – business studies). It was a point-in-time study (Column 6 – point in time).

7.4 Final comments

This work has demonstrated the rich array of emprical EAP linguistic inquiry over recent decades. The inquiry has resulted in a substantial body of description of academic English that is now available. This book presented only a limited amount of the description available in the EAP literature in the Studies in Focus sections and to report simply on the methodologies in the often-complex forms inquiries the studies involved. It was the aim of these sections to showcase the kind of inquiries that have characterised linguistic research in EAP. The present work was motivated by the desire that the reach and impact of the inquiry and description could be extended to an audience beyond the EAP community. Researchers in education, teachers in school settings and university disciplinary teachers and researchers may have interests in the language choices typically used to convey subject content and express ideas and the conventionalised patterns of regularly occurring educational and research genres and events. Within Applied Linguistics, researchers in other specialisms such as SLA or curriculum studies may draw on this body of literature.

In any field of inquiry, it can be useful from time to time to stand back and assess research endeavours. This kind of assessment is seen in two important recent EAP publications (Hyland & Jiang, in press; Swales, 2019). In the present Final Comments section, I would like to identify two particularly strong lines of EAP linguistic inquiry to date. Research activities that appear to have been very fruitful are genre-based research into specific genres or part genres, corpus-based inquires in the general academic English register and studies of disciplinary varieties of academic English. Genre-based inquiries have provided "pedagogically applicable" descriptions (Swales, 2019: 77) of great value to teachers, learners and researchers, and nowhere is this more the case than in inquiries into written academic genres. Studies have revealed regularly occurring structural patterns, or typified ways of organising genres or events. Genre analysis brings to light what people are doing when they are speaking or writing as analysis focuses on the communicative purposes of moves and can be especially insightful if analysis goes beyond the texts (the genre samples) to interviewing those who produce or receive the genres (Swales, 2019). Corpus analysis brings

Conclusion and Future Directions 99

to light what linguistic items or patterns are typically used and can be combined with other research measures to identify items for "possible or potential pedagogical uptake" (Swales, 2019: 77).

One area that I would suggest for further theoretical inquiry in EAP is the topic of implicit and explicit knowledge of academic English. This topic was introduced and discussed in Chapter 2. The descriptions of academic English presented in the chapters of this book are empirical studies of discourse in academic, educational or research settings. In recent decades, scholars have generally conceptualised academic English as conventionalised patterns and choices of disciplinary (professional) groups. Swales (1990) developed the highly influential notion of academic discourse communities that underlies much empirical inquiry in recent decades. Hyland (2011: 184) describes the role discourse analysis plays in providing insights into how academics and students create understanding "as members of professional groups, revealing something of how their discoursal decisions are socially grounded in the knowledge structures and rhetorical repertoires of their disciplines." When we examine discourse practices we examine texts, the products of the discoursal decisions. But where does the knowledge to make such decisions come from? How do members of academic discourse communities tap into community-held rhetorical repertoires, and are these repertoires to be construed as forms of explicit or implicit linguistic knowledge? These are topics for future inquiry.

References

Basturkmen, H. (2003). So, what happens when the tutor walks in? Some observations on interaction in a university discussion group with and without the tutor. *Journal of English for Academic Purposes*, 2: 21–33.

Basturkmen, H. (2012). A genre-based investigation of discussion sections in research articles in dentistry and disciplinary variation. *Journal of English for Academic Purposes*, 11(2): 134–144.

Camiciottoli, B.C. (2020). The OpenCourseWare lecture: A new twist on an old genre? *Journal of English for Academic Purposes*, 46.

Coxhead, A., Parkinson, J., Mackay, J., & Mc Laughlin, E. (2019). *English for vocational purposes: Language use in trades education*. London: Routledge.

Hu, G. & Liu, Y. (2018). Three-minute thesis presentations as an academic genre: A cross-disciplinary study of genre moves. *Journal of English for Academic Purposes*, 35: 16–30.

Hyland, K. (2011). Academic discourse. In K. Hyland & B. Paltridge (Eds), *The Bloomsbury companion to discourse analysis* (pp. 171–184). London: Bloomsbury.

Hyland, K. & Jiang, F. (in press). A bibliographic study of EAP research: Who is doing what, where and when? *Journal of English for Academic Purposes.*
Nesi, H. & Gardner, S. (2012). *Genres across the disciplines: Student writing in higher education.* Cambridge: Cambridge University Press.
Paltridge, B. (2006). *Discourse analysis.* London: Continuum.
Parkinson, J. (2019). Multimodal student texts: Implications for ESP. In K. Hyland & L.L.C. Wong (Eds) *Specialised English: New directions in ESP and EAP research and practice* (pp. 149–161). London: Routledge.
Swales, J.M. (1990). *Genre analysis: English in academic and research settings.* Cambridge: Cambridge University Press.
Swales, J.M. (2019). The future of EAP genre studies: A personal viewpoint. *Journal of English for Academic Purposes*, 38: 75–82.
Tusting, K., McCulloch, S., Bhatt, I. Hamilton, M. & Barton, D. (2019). *Academics writing: The dynamics of knowledge creation.* London: Routledge.
Wingate, U. (2012). "Argument!" helping students understand what essay writing is about. *Journal of English for Academic Purposes*, 11: 145–154.

Index

Note: Page numbers in *italics* indicate figures and in **bold** indicate tables on the corresponding pages.

academic formulas 41–43, **42**, **43**
academic idioms 43–44, **44**
academic word families 40–41
Academic Word List (AWL) 40–41
adverbials of result 84
Appel, R. 52
Applied Linguistics 1

Bardetta, V. S. 38
Basturkmen, H. 6, 57–59, *58*, 81–82, 98
Becher, T. 85
Bennet, K. 35
Biber, D. 37
Black, S. 38
Bloor, M. 18, 81
Bloor, T. 18, 81
British Academic Spoken English (BASE) 44, 55, 95
British National Corpus (BNC) 42
Bruce, I. 48, 84

CARS (Create a research space) model 66, 73
case reports 84
Chang, Y.-Y. 84–85
Charles, M. 67
Chiu Y.-L. 51
Classification Framework for Inquiry and Description of Academic English 96–98, **97**
Cohen, L. 15

common core, general English 18, *19*
communicative competence 15
community of practice 80
comparative genre analysis 83–84
conference proposals 68–69
Connor, U. M. 68–69
corpus analysis 27
Coxhead, A. 40–41, 52, 96
Csomay, E. 52

Dang, T. N. Y. 52
Deroey, K. L. B. 55–57, *56*
dialogue 57
disciplinary variation, EAP linguistic inquiry: changing patterns of disciplinary meta discourse in 86–88, *87*; discipline-specific phrase lists for secondary school 88–90, **89**; importance of 79–82; introduction to 78–79; nature of 83–85; studies on 85–90; three-minute thesis presentations 85–86, **86**
discipline-specific phrase lists for secondary school 88–90, **89**
Discipline-Specific Writing: Theory into Practice 1
discourse analysis 21–25, *22*, *24*, **25**; academic registers, events and genres in 24–25, **25**
discussion class interaction 57–59, *58*
Dressen-Hammouda, D. 83

Index

El-Dakhs, D. A. S. 68
Ellis, N. C. 41–42
English, learning of academic: learning needs and relevance of descriptions 9, **10**; targets of 20–21; views of 17–20, *19*
English as an additional language (EAL) 64–65
English for Academic Purposes (EAP) linguistic inquiry: classification framework for 96–98, **97**; contexts of 7–9; definition of 5–7, *6*; directions for future 93–96; disciplinary variation (*see* disciplinary variation, EAP linguistic inquiry); final comments on 98–99; historical antecedents and growing importance of 3–5; introduction to 1–3; professional research genres and events and (*see* genres and events, professional research); strands of *6*, 6–7; study genres and events and (*see* genres and events, study); summary and overview of 9–11; theory and methodology (*see* theory and methodology, EAP linguistic inquiry)
English for General Academic Purposes (EGAP) *6*, 6–7, 19–20, 81; importance of description in 34–35
English for Instructional Purposes (EIP) *6*, 6–7
English for Professional Academic Purposes (EPAP) *6*, *6*, 63
English for Research Publication Purposes (ERPP) *6*, 6–7, 63
English for Specific Academic Purposes (ESAP) *6*, 6–7, 19–20; importance of description in 34–35
English for Study Purposes *6*, *6*
English Language Teaching (ELT) 1, 3
English Medium Instruction (EMI) 2–3, 4–5; targets of 8
evaluation strategies in research article introductions 72–74, *73*
Evans, S. 84

exchange structure 58–59
explicit knowledge 28–30, *29*

field accounts 83
Flowerdew, J. 64, 84
Forest, R. W. 84
formal style in academic writing 37–38, **38**
formulas, academic 41–43, **42**, **43**

Gardner, S. 51, 52–55, **53**, *54*
Ge, G.-c. 84
general academic English register: academic formulas and 41–43, **42**, **43**; academic idioms and 43–44, **44**; academic word families and 40–41; features associated with informal style and 38–39, **40**; formal style in academic writing and 37–38, **38**; importance of description of 34–35; introduction to 33–34; nature of description of 35–36; studies of 36–44
General Service List (GSL) 40–41
genre analysis 16–17, 24–25, **25**; comparative 83–84; qualitative analysis in 26
Genres across Disciplines: Student Writing 84
genres and events: professional research: comparative inquiry in 67–68; conference proposals 68–69; evaluation strategies in research article introductions 72–74, *73*; importance of 63–65; introduction to 62–63; merging move and corpus analysis 68; nature of inquiry in 65–68; question-and-answer sessions at end of conference presentations 69–72, *70*, **71–72**; research article as contested term in 66–67; studies of 68–74; terrain of 67–68; study: discussion class interaction and 57–59, *58*; functions in lecturer talk and 55–57, *56*; general academic registers and 24–25, **25**; importance of description of 47–49, **48**; introduction to 46–47, **47**; nature of description of 49–52, **50**;

student genres of assessed writing 52–55, **53**, *54*; studies of 52–59
grammatical compression structures 37–38, **38**
Gray, B. 37
Green, C. 8, 88–90, **89**

Halleck, G. B. 68–69
Hamp-Lyons, L. 83
Hewings, A. 36
Holmes, R. 83
Hu, G. 85–86, **86**
Hyland, K. 17, 36, 79, 81, 83, 94, 99; changing patterns of disciplinary meta discourse 86–88, *87*
Hymes, D. 15

idioms, academic 43–44, **44**
implicit knowledge 29–30, 35, 82
implicit learning 30
informal style 38–39, **40**
introduction-Method-Result-Discussion (IMRD) pattern 84
Irvine, A. 7

Jiang, F. K. 86–88, *87*, 94
Johnstone, B. 23, 24
John Swales Conference Corpus (JSCC) 71–72, **71–72**
Journal of English for Academic Purposes 1, 83

Keller, K. 69–72, *70*, **71–72**

Lambert, J. 8; discipline-specific phrase lists for secondary school 88–90, **89**
Lau, K. 47
lecturer talk, functions in 55–57, *56*
Liang, S.-l. 84
Liardét, C. L. 38–39
Lillis, T. 36
Lim, J. M. H. 83
Lin, C.-Y. 47
Lin, L. 84
linguistic analysis *22*, 22–23
linguistic inquiry *see* English for Academic Purposes (EAP) linguistic inquiry

Liu, Y. 85–86, **86**
Loi, C. K. 67

Malmström, H. 7
Manion, L. 15
Matheson, N. 81–82
Matzler, P. 65
Mayor, B. 36
Medical Academic Word List 84
meta discourse, disciplinary 86–88, *87*
Michigan Corpus of Academic Spoken English (MICASE) 42, 95
Miller, J. 43–44

Nation, I. S. P. 40
Nesi, H. 51; evaluation strategies in research article introductions 72–74, *73*; student genres of assessed writing 52–55, **53**, *54*
New Academic Word List (AWL) 40–41

O'Boyle, A. 52
Ogiermann, E. 47
orientations: product-oriented and process-oriented 65–66; social 23–24, *24*
Oxford Corpus of Academic English (OCAE) 44

Paltridge, B. 65, 97
Parkinson, J. 51, 96
Pecorari, D. 7, 67
Power, K. 66–67
process-oriented research 65–66
product-oriented research 65–66
Pun, J. K. H. 51

question-and-answer sessions at end of conference presentations 69–72, *70*, **71–72**

research articles (RA) 66–67; evaluation strategies in 72–74, *73*
Routledge Handbook of English for Academic Purposes 1

Second Language Acquisition (SLA) 2
Seliger, H. W. 26

Shaw, P. 7, 36
Sheldon, E. 67
Shohamy, E. 26
Simpson-Vlach, R. 41–42
society orientation 23–24, *24*
Starfield, S. 65
Structure of Technical English, The 20
Swales, J. 16–17, 20, 51, 69, 99; CARS (Create a research space) model 66, 73; on disciplinary variation 85; question-and-answer sessions at end of conference presentations 69–72, *70*, **71–72**; on rhetorical structure genre analysis 95

tacitly-held knowledge 28–30, *29*
Tardy, C. M. 65
Tarone, E. 81
Taverniers, M. A. 55–57, *56*
theory and methodology, EAP linguistic inquiry: academic registers, events and genres in 24–25, **25**; discourses and texts in 21–23, *22*; introduction to 14; making tacitly-held knowledge explicit 28–30, *29*; orientations in 23–24, *24*; variable methodological options in 25–28; views of language 15–21, *19*
three-minute thesis presentations 85–86, **86**
Tusting, K. 96

University Word List (UWL) 40

van Enk, A. 66–67

Wang, J. 84
Wells, G. 80
West, M. 41
Wingate, U. 47
Wood, D. C. 52
word families, academic 40–41
Wulff, S. 69–72, *70*, **71–72**

Xu, X. 72–74, *73*
Xue, G. 40

Zanina, E. 67
Zareva, A. 52

For Product Safety Concerns and Information please contact our EU representative GPSR@taylorandfrancis.com
Taylor & Francis Verlag GmbH, Kaufingerstraße 24, 80331 München, Germany

www.ingramcontent.com/pod-product-compliance
Lightning Source LLC
Chambersburg PA
CBHW070559170426
43201CB00012B/1881